You *Can* Train Your Dog; Mastering the Art & Science of Modern Dog Training

by Pamela Dennison, CDBC

GW00645429

SHADOW PUBLISHING
Published by Shadow Publishing,
34 Lakeview Ave, Blairstown, New Jersey, 07825 U.S.A.

You Can Train Your Dog; Mastering the Art & Science of Modern Dog Training and Design are registered trademarks of Shadow Publishing and Pamela Dennison.

International Standard Book Number: 978-0-9966655-0-6
Library of Congress Catalog Card Number: 2015948198
Printed in the United States of America

Front cover image © Pamela Dennison.
Back cover image © Animal Photography

Note: This publication contains the opinions and ideas of its author. It is intended to provide helpful and informative material on the subject matter covered. It is sold with the understanding that the author and publisher are not engaged in rendering professional services in the book. If the reader requires personal assistance or advice, a competent professional should be consulted.

The author and publisher specifically disclaim any responsibility for any liability, loss, or risk, personal or otherwise, which is incurred as a consequence, directly or indirectly, of the use and application of any of the contents of this book.

Publisher: Shadow Publishing
Executive Editors: Jill Kessler Miller and Pamela Dennison
Graphic Design: www.PawsInk.com
Photographers: Pamela Dennison, Terri Hirsch, Samantha Staino and Emmanuel Jaborska

To U-CD Commander Cody's Great Escape, CGC, A-CD, CDX, NJC, October 18, 1992–June 6, 2005, my "crossover" dog: Sorry it took so long for me to find positive training, and thank you for being such a patient dog.

To my dogs "at the bridge" who reaped the benefit of what I learned with Cody:

To ARCHEX Ewe Are Beyond a Shadow of a Doubt, CGC, CD, TD, TSW, NA, NAJ. May 17, 1999 - December 24, 2012

A-UD, ARCHEX, Surely Ewe Beau Jest, CGC, TDI, CD, NAJP, NAP, TSW, RLV. July 1, 1998 - April 19, 2014

And of course to my existing dogs who at this printing are:

A-UD, UD-C, ARCHX Emma Ewe Found Me, RL3, CGC, CDX, TSW
ARCH Finnish What Ewe Started, CGC, BN, CD, CDX-C, RL3
ARCH Pinnacle Dream a Little Dream of Ewe, CGC, CD-C, RL1X, RL3

Punishment is like a nuclear bomb;
If the blast doesn't get you,
The fallout will.
Steve White

Table of Contents

Foreward   13
Introduction   15
Acknowledgements   17

Chapter 1: **Modern Training Fundamentals   19**

Clicker Training   19
The Three Laws of Learning   21
      The First Law of Learning   22
      The Second Law of Learning   22
      The Third Law of Learning   22
Reinforcing What You Like   23
Ignoring What You Don't Like   24
Breaking Down Each Behavior Into Tiny Pieces   24
Keep Sessions Short and Successful   25
Fixing Bad Behaviors By Reinforcing Good Ones   26
The Positives of Modern Training   26
Pop Quiz   28

Chapter 2: **10 Myths of Positive Training Dispelled   31**

Myth #1: The Clicker Is a Fad or Gimmick   31
Myth #2: The Principles Are Too Difficult to Learn and to Understand   31
Myth #3: Positive Reinforcement Takes Too Long   32
Myth #4: In Training, a Dog Should Never Be Given a Choice   33
Myth #5: You Must Always Have the Clicker with You   33
Myth #6: Clicker-Trained Dogs Won't Work Without Food   33
Myth #7: Force Works Better   34
Myth #8: Positive Training Isn't Effective with Barking or Aggression   34
Myth #9: You Must Be Dominant to Your Dog   35
Myth #10: TV shows are real life   36
Pop Quiz   37

Chapter 3: **Are You Listening to What Your Dog is Telling You?   37**

Why Dogs Give Off Calming Signals   39
Understanding Your Dog's Signals   40
Is Your Dog Stressed?   41
Stressed-Out Puppies   42
Stress for Adult Dogs   42

A Brand-New Language: What the 50 Dog Signals Are   43
    Calming   43
    Stress   43
Ambiguous Signals   50
Personal Stress Signals   52
Body Language That May Stress Your Dog   54
Ways That You Can Reduce Your Dog's Stress   56
How Will Knowing Your Dog's Signals Help You Train Him?   57
Growling   58
Stopping Bad Behaviors in Stressful Situations   59
Strangers   59
Leashes   60
Set Up For Success   61
Homework   61
Pop Quiz   62

Chapter 4: **The ABCs of Learning**   63

The Basis of All Learning   63
A Is for Antecedent   64
B Is for Behavior   64
C Is for Consequence   64
The Four Main Principles of Operant Conditioning   65
    Positive Reinforcement   66
    Positive Punishment   66
    Negative Reinforcement   67
    Negative Punishment   67
Classical Conditioning (Associative Learning)   68
Why Is Classical Conditioning Used?   68
Bad Associations   69
Keeping Those Good Associations Happenin'   69
Pop Quiz   70

Chapter 5: **Foundation Skills**   71

Just Say No to "No"   71
Begin at the Beginning   72
What is a Learned Behavior?   72
It All Starts With Eye Contact   74
My Name Is "No, No, Bad Dog!"—What's Yours?   75
Praise Words   76
The First Stage of "Come"   76
Sit, Down, Stand   77
Pop Quiz   85

Chapter 6: **Verbal and Whistle Recall** **87**

Recall: The "basic recipe" 87
Priming the whistle 88
The "Drop-the-Cookie-and-Run-Like-Heck" Game 88
"Drop the cookie and don't run" game 90
The "Let your dog get distracted" game 91
The "Liar's Game" 91
Play Hide-and-Seek 93
Walking in a Field or Trail 93
What if my dog doesn't respond? 94
Adding Distractions 94
Pop Quiz 96

Chapter 7: **Animal Husbandry** **97**

Petting and Handling 97
"Collar" (noun) 100
"Collar" (verb) 101
Leash and "collar" 101
"Collar" (lead) 101
Scruff (lead) 101
Belly 102
Brushing and touching 102
One foot, two foot, green foot, blue foot 103
Toe nails 105
"Settle" and "Roll Over" 105

Chapter 8: **Loose Leash Walking** **109**

Why Dogs Pull 109
Because We Follow 110
To Get to the Other Side 110
Opposition Reflex 111
Building an Outdoor Relationship 111
Be the "Stupid Bunny" 112
Moving Backups 114
Pivot to heel 115
Heeling games 116
"This way" 116
Automatic sit 116
Call front 116
Follow the Leader 117
Loose-Leash Walking 118

Automatic check-in   118
Automatic check-in with name/come response   118
Click the leash, not the dog!   119
Does "be a tree" really work?   119
Turning Your Worst Distraction into Your Greatest Ally   119
"I'm with you, you're with me" Dance   120
Pop Quiz   121

Chapter 9: **Teaching the Stays**   **123**

"Sit," "Down," and "Stand Stay"   123
Door Etiquette   124
Adding Distractions to the Stay and All Other Behaviors   127
Wait a Minute!   127
Go to Your Mat!   127
Waiting for Dinner   129
Pop Quiz   130

Chapter 10: **Puppy Socialization**   **131**

Properly Socialize   131
Watch Carefully For Signs of Stress   132
Places for Socialization   132
To Home School or Not to Home School   133
Is One Class Enough?   133
How About Dog Parks?   134
Strangers   134
The Environment   135
Doggie Food Bowls   135
Crate Training   136
The Benefits of Crate Training   137
Crate-Training Instructions   138
The Bathroom Is Outside   140
Knowing When to Go   140
False Alarms and Accidents   142
Play Time   142
Pop Quiz   143

Chapter 11: **Self Control Games**   **145**

The two toy game   145
Building toy drive   146
Tug of war   147
Rev up and cool down   147
"Mine" a.k.a. Leave it   148

Chapter 12: **Slots, Soda and Hawaii: Reinforcements** **153**

It's a Shell Game: Different Reinforcement Schedules   153
Continuous Reinforcement   153
Fixed Schedule of Reinforcement Slows Down Learning   153
Eenie, Meenie, Minie, Mo: Variable Reinforcement   154
When the Soda Machine Suddenly Becomes a Slot Machine   155
Eureka! Variable Reinforcement   155
Variety: The Spice of Your Dog's Life   156
Pack Your Bags—We're Going to Hawaii!: Adding Surprise Elements   157
Pop Quiz   158

Chapter 13: **Manipulation Modern Style; The Premark Principle** **159**

Eat Your Vegetables First: What You Want   159
Hot Fudge Sundae: What Does Your Dog Want?   159
Becoming a Master Manipulator   160
Added Benefits   161
Green Means Stop, Red Means Go: Giving Consistent Cues   162
Pop Quiz   162

Chapter 14: **What if My Dog Makes a Mistake** **165**

Proceed, Putting It on Cue   166
    Proceed: Moving On to Something Else   166
    Putting It on Cue   167
Management, Aid, Antecedent   167
    Aid   168
    Antecedent   168
Incompatible, Ignore, Innovation   168
    Ignoring the Dog   169
    Innovation   170
Repeat, Redirect, Recreation, Restrain   170
    Redirect   170
    Recreation   171
    Restrain   171
Pop Quiz   172

Chapter 15: **Positive Solutions to "Bad" Behavior** **173**

One Dog's Punishment Is Another's Reinforcement   173
Suppression   173
Barking   174
    Almost Sure-Fire Way to Minimize Barking: "Uncle Fred"   175

Alert Barking   175
Jumping   175
Solutions for jumping   176
    Go Visit (a.k.a. The Two Trainer Game)   176
    Person Approaching = Sit   177
    Excuse Me   177
Nipping and mouthing   178
Biting the Kids   179
Can Dogs Really Have Selective Deafness?   180
Pop Quiz   181

Chapter 16: **Side Effects of Punishment   183**

What Is Punishment?   183
Escalating Punishment   184
Observable Effects of Punishment   184
Causes of "Bad" Behaviors   185
Anxiety and Fear   186
Escape and Avoidance   188
Aggression   189
Types and Causes of Aggression   190
Learned Helplessness   191
Pop Quiz   192

Chapter 17: **Incorporating Training Into Your Life   193**

Creating Creative Training Sessions   193
Training Goals   195
Incorporating Training into Your Routine   195
An Apple a Day   196
Sample Training Guides   196
Where All This Fun Might Lead You   200
    Therapy Dog   200
    Rally   200
    Competition Obedience   201
    Agility   202
    Sheep Herding   202
    Musical Freestyle   203
    Treibball   204
    Nosework   204
    Other Sports   204
Pop Quiz   206

Chapter 18: **The Canine Good Citizen Test   207**

Accepting a Friendly Stranger   207
Sitting Politely for Petting   208
Appearance and Grooming   208
Heeling/Loose leash walking; Out for a walk   209
Walking Through a Crowd   210
Sit, down, stay   210
Coming When Called   211
Reaction to Distractions   211
Reaction to Another Dog   212
Supervised separation   214

Appendix   217

Foreword

After 25 years of reading, researching, and applying animal training to an assortment of finned, flippered, feathered, and furred critters—from whales to walruses, from dolphins to dogs—I can confidently state that it's finally here: a succinct guide to dog training that explains the often-confusing and complex science of animal learning in simple terms.

Dogs are remarkable animals capable of learning a variety of complex behaviors if owners commit a little time each day and train in small steps using patience and understanding. When they are rewarded for each of these small steps, dogs can learn as fast as dolphins, chimpanzees, or even killer whales. For new pet owners, however, training always seems easiest right before they actually bring the new dog home to live. How hard could it be to teach a "Sit," or to walk calmly on a leash, or basic potty training? That is until you realize that the wet spot on the rug is not water, that the neighbors really don't appreciate barking at 2:00 a.m., and that a "let's go" is supposed to cue your new pet to walk forward and not to go in reverse. As we often learn, what seems simple can get awfully complicated.

Pam Dennison has been a tireless advocate for positive, productive, and enriching training methods, most of which she has outlined in this guide. As a dog-training instructor and award-winning obedience trainer, Pam has patiently guided dog owners so that they might better understand the process of reducing unwanted behavior in a positive and productive way, while maintaining a trusting relationship with their pet. At the same time, she also teaches dog owners how to shape new behaviors such as basic obedience, potty training, and proper socialization with children. Advanced trainers have also benefited from Pam's expertise, especially in competition obedience training, where her skills are most obvious.

But most notably, she has enough confidence in her personal-training knowledge and applied skills to take on some extreme behavior challenges using the same techniques outlined in the following pages. The results have been remarkable. Her success with a highly aggressive Border Collie named "Shadow" has been a shining example of training excellence that quite literally changed Shadow's life. The training that Shadow received transformed him from a severely aggressive and reactive animal to a well-trained and well-mannered pet. Even more remarkable, Shadow is now competing in registered trials and doing excellent!

The rewards of dog ownership become evident when animals are taught behaviors that help them live comfortably and confidently in the household. The relationship between a family and their pet is further strengthened when fascinating behaviors are trained that highlight their pet's intelligence and personality. Finally, true miracles are accomplished when owners learn how to change behaviors in a way that positively impacts the quality of life for animals challenged with overcoming fear, anxiety, phobias, and aggression.

In a very practical way, this guide addresses many of these areas and has synthesized the multitude of training techniques into a helpful tool, complete with real examples, entertaining stories, and valuable training exercises. The rest is up to you. Stay positive and keep the training fun!
—Ted Turner, Animal Behaviorist

Introduction

Thank you for choosing to train your best friend using the most proven and updated techniques! Modern dog training has been proven by behavioral psychologists to be the most effective way to train and maintain any behavior. As you will see, punishment causes toxic side effects and can harm your relationship with your dog. There are many, many ways to let your dog know that you don't like his behavior without punishing or yelling at him.

I think the biggest difference between modern dog training and traditional dog training is this; when one removes as much force as is safe for the animal and handler, it builds a whole repertoire of reinforcers. One can't use force and expect an animal to not be frightened into protection mode.

When I started training, I went to a "traditional" punishment-based training class. After a while, I was seeing a decrease of "good" behaviors and an increase of "bad" behaviors with my dogs. They started to hate training and I was angry all of the time.

I was at a standstill in my training for competition because the only advice given in traditional training was to use more and harsher punishment. This made no sense to me and I went on a learning quest, found positive training, "crossed over," and started my business, Positive Motivation Dog Training, in 1996.

For those of you who have trained a dog using traditional methods, it may take a while for you to get the hang of not being heavy handed, but you will see faster results and then be hooked, just like I was!

Acknowledgements

My undying gratitude goes to Kenya Ebersole and Joanne Woodward for their help in so many ways, to my editor Jill Kessler Miller and my designer, Rebeccah Aube and always, to Ted Turner.

And for those people that don't even know me, but who had a major impact on my life; Leslie Nelson, Bob Bailey and Turid Rugaas.

For those of you that had faith in this project and helped out financially to make this book come to life. I couldn't have done it without you all! It does take a village! Ellen Griffith, Diane Boyd, Virginia Wind, Sarah Woodruff, John McCormick, Maryanne Shaffer VanSaders, Kirsten Murphy, Venita Bentley, Lola Carey, Jim Dennison, Tom & Ann Fischer, Nadine Cressman, Laurel Pearson, Susan Vaitekunas, Abigail Christman, Charlene Schreiber, Kathy Scali, Donna Kemp, Janine Krystofosky, Caroline Wolstenholme, Deb Manheim, Sarah Morris, Inge Noeninger, Tracy Weber, Roberta Kublin, Carol Brynes, Esther Williams, Kathy Schwabe, AJ Eller, Deb Knappenberger, Laura Ashtyani, Cathy Hivner, Gabrielle Milford, Susan Kennedy, Kristen White, Shirley J. Comins, Delia Quigley, Jennifer Mauger, Debra Harner, Rhonea Bellon, Jayne Berman Dubin, Bianca Falbo, Kenya Ebersole, Karen Profenna, Denise St. John, Jonathon Buggey, Nikki Verhof, Joe & Theresa Patrick, Sandra Cox, Karen Wylie, Michelle Howard, Kelly Ernewein-Stilson, Lindsay Mcfadden, Lynn Adams, Elaine Booker, James Longo, Denise DeGeyter, Leigh Shannon, Josh Allen, Helen Hargett, Katie Casell, Gailanne Antonicello, Leslie Sherman, Tracie Jones-Davies, Gopakumar Menon, Chantal Cartier, Melodee Lasky, Pat Dalrymple, Nancy Brunswick, Wendy Eld, Katja Mechler, Diane Herbert Zdrodowski, Barb Sahl, Jayne Lips, Diana Boos, Michelle Curran, Joyce Gauthier, Bonnie Weimer Poirier, Jane Stride, Gina Boderck, Marguerite Plank, Kathleen Gardosh, Stacy Braslau-Schneck, Margery Cavins, Michelle Cerone, Donald Centner, Debby McMullen, Joanne Sheffler, Annette MacNair, Peggy McCallum, Elana Smith, Kate Pleasance, and Astrid Smith.

And to the dogs: Cody, Beau, Shadow, Mollie, Carrie, Brandy, Noel, Emma, Finn and Dreamer.

To my mother, Zelda Gross, who said, "Of course you can do it."

Modern Training Fundamentals 1

Modern training is precise manipulation of favorable consequences (such as food, play and toys) in order to teach your dog to respond with the behaviors you want. Behavioral psychology studies demonstrate that positive training is successful under the most rigorous conditions, proving that the methodology in this book is not "just one person's opinion."

"Positive" doesn't equal "permissive." My happy dogs are subject to strict rules and regulations regarding their behavior around the house and proper manners when away from home. Physical or verbal punishments are unnecessary.

Clicker Training

Clicker training is only one facet of positive training; the "click" signals the dog that he did something right. A clicker is simply a marker signal—a specific sound that marks the correct behavior the instant the dog performs it. The clicker doesn't train your dog — you still have to engage your dog, but using a clicker as a marker signal can both enhance and speed up your training. The clicker itself is a small plastic box with a metal tongue that when pressed creates a "click" sound. They can be found in most larger pet and dog-equipment stores.

Clicker training (I use the terms "positive training and clicker training" interchangeably in this book) teaches dogs to think and to use the wonderful, creative brains they possess. It also gives them some control. By "control," I don't mean in a dominating, pushy, bossy way, but in a way that brings their own abilities and willingness into the training process, because you've created a safe environment for him. Once you start training using the clicker, you'll see that your dog isn't working just for the food—he's working to get you to click, creating an exchange of communication.

The clicker also imparts valuable information to the trainer. When trying to mark behavior with words, such as the ever-popular "good dog," it's difficult to know whether or not we're marking the behavior we actually want. More often than not, we're late with our mark (click), and need to work on fixing our timing. If you are continuously late or ill-timed with your verbal "good dog,"you will probably experience dogs that seem confused and simply not "getting it." If that happens, just step back, rethink, readjust and redo.

The Science

*If you don't want to use a clicker, that's
fine with me. However, to be an effective
trainer and create a dog who's a fast
learner, you must use some sort of marker
signal — otherwise he won't have a clue
what you're reinforcing. Other markers
can include a clucking mouth sound, a
whistle (do not use a whistle as a marker*

> **Alert!**
> Be careful about using a flash of light
> unless you have no other choice. These
> kinds of toys (laser pointers) can create
> shadow chasing, an OCD behavior that is
> very difficult to get rid of.

*signal if you plan on training a whistle recall!), a flash of light, a thumbs up (like I
use with deaf dogs).*

The strength and beauty of modern training is it takes the onus off of the dog and
puts it squarely where it belongs—on us. The dog is never wrong. Really. We're the
teachers. We're the ones in the driver's seat. When we make a wrong turn and get
lost, we can't blame the person next to us because we're the ones holding the wheel.

Be aware that a few correct repetitions does not a learned behavior make. Just
because your dog was able to perform a behavior once or twice doesn't mean that it's
learned or reliable. And even if the dog does a wrong behavior, so what? We all make
mistakes or do stupid things—even when we know better. I'm allergic to certain
foods, but I eat them anyway. Dogs can be just as silly or capricious as we are; don't
take it personally!

Step-by-step instructions for using a clicker for teaching specific behaviors are
addressed in Chapters 5, 7, 9, 11.

The Science

A Short Bit of History

*Ivan Pavlov (1849–1936) is the man who gave us Pavlovian conditioning, also called
classical conditioning. You remember Pavlov with the dog, the bell, and the drool?
Pavlov learned through his research that if he paired a neutral stimulus (a bell —
something that previously had no meaning for the dog) with meat powder, after a few
repetitions, the dog would drool upon hearing the bell. And thus associative learning
was created. Associations are the first steps to learning anything, which will be
important in later lessons addressed in this book.*

*B.F. Skinner (1904–1990) was a forerunner in the study of operant conditioning,
secondary reinforcers, and ratios of reinforcement. (For more information, see
Chapter 12.) He discovered that changes in behavior are a result of the individual's
response (observable behavior) to the events happening in the environment. In other
words, when you can observe a change in behavior, learning has occurred. You are
no longer allowed to think or say "But he knows what I want!" because learning is
the outcome of change in observable behaviors.*

"Observable behavior" is key here because if you can't perceive a change in behavior (for better or worse), then you can't assume that learning has actually occurred. We can't read our dog's mind, but we can learn to observe them more closely. Once we do that, we can adjust our training to effect desired behavior changes.

The Three Laws of Learning

There are a few simple rules in using positive methods. They may sound too simplistic to really be effective, but it's true. Once you learn the reasoning and the nuances of modern training, it becomes more natural and second nature.

No matter which method you use, be it positive reinforcement or punishment-based methods, the laws of learning remain the same. It doesn't make any difference if you're training a dog, person, cat, or horse. Although they are all widely diverse in many areas, including modes of communicating, social needs, desires, and basic fundamental drives, they all have one thing in common: all are obedient to the laws of learning.

The three basic laws are the following:
- Rewarded behavior is repeated.
- Ignored behavior stops.
- Once a behavior is in place, random (variable) rewards will strengthen the behavior.

The Science
No matter which method you use, be it positive reinforcement or punishment-based methods, the laws of learning remain the same.

If you've noticed, I never said the behaviors strengthened would be good ones. We have this bizarre human tendency to reinforce the very behavior we don't want. Dog jumps, we knee him in the chest; dog pulls, we jerk back; dog barks, we yell. Part of my job with this book is to teach you how to properly reinforce what you do want and how to properly and effectively ignore what you don't. As with everything, there is a right and a wrong way to do both.

Let's say you continually leave food on the counter and your dog has been successful (rewarded) many times for stealing it. Now you decide to keep your counters spotlessly clean, and after a long time, your dog never even thinks about jumping up to steal some food. Then for about a week or so, you're very busy, forget to put the food away, and your dog is taking food off the counter again. Then you go back to putting the food away, but because your dog has now been randomly reinforced for jumping on the counter, that behavior may become very strong.

The First Law of Learning
Behavior that is rewarded is most likely to be repeated:

Your dog jumps all over you when you come home wearing a clean suit. You pay attention to him (either positively or negatively), and he will continue to do the same behavior whenever you come home.

You might wonder how negative attention (yelling or hitting) could be rewarding for the dog. If the only time you interact with your dog is to tell him what he did wrong, then he'll continue to do those very behaviors. Sounds pretty darned crazy, doesn't it? But to the dog, being yelled at may be preferable to being ignored. Or it may be that your dog thinks you're playing with him. We all know dogs that do that — race around, staying out of reach, while we turn purple.

The Second Law of Learning
Behavior that is not reinforced, over time, will most likely stop (extinguish):

You come home, your dog starts to jump all over you, and you now ignore him for about 10 minutes until he relaxes, and then you pay attention to him.

Now when you come home, he will lie down and relax until you come over to greet him.

Personal example: I was having a similar issue with my two Shelties, so I started to leave a container of treats in my hallway. Before they started to bark, I tossed some treats into the living room. That kept them quiet long enough so I could get in the house and they in turn, learned that quiet behavior got them attention. They also weren't letting me in bed at night — they were bouncing all over the bed so that I couldn't pull the covers back and barking, barking, barking. Then I remembered, "Oh right, I'm a dog trainer, I can fix this." So I brought some treats into the bedroom and asked them to sit and stay on the floor as I got into bed. If they stayed, I tossed them treats. After only two nights of training this new incompatible behavior, they now wait patiently on the floor until I invite them up on the bed, without the use of treats.

There may come a time where an inappropriate behavior your dog is exhibiting is very self-reinforcing to your dog, so ignoring won't work. Many other positive strategies you can utilize are in Chapter 15.

The Third Law of Learning
Once a behavior is established, a variable (unpredictable to the dog) schedule of reinforcement will make the behavior stronger:

You come home and are now wearing old clothes, so you allow the dog to jump on you, but you continue to ignore the dog when you're wearing a suit.

Guess what? Your dog isn't a fashion critic and will continue to jump all over you when you come home, because you have variably (sometimes yes and sometimes no) reinforced the jumping.

Reinforcing What You Like

Many people don't know what they want in terms of their dog's behavior. If you don't know what you want, then you won't recognize it when you get it! "I just want a good dog" doesn't count. You may want a dog that doesn't pull on the leash or jump on strangers or try to set his own place at the dinner table. Learn to be more specific.

Make a list of the behaviors you observe in your dog now, along with what you'd rather see instead. Here are some examples:

Existing Behavior	What You Want Instead
Jumping on strangers	Sitting politely for petting
Pulling on the leash	Walking calmly by my side
Barking at the doorbell	Quiet when doorbell rings
Bucking bronco for grooming	Standing still for grooming
Growling at strangers	Watching strangers calmly

Once you've identified what you want, you'll be surprised at how often you actually do get these behaviors—even without training. No dog can be "bad" 24 hours a day, seven days a week. Really. Not even yours. And now you can start watching for the "good" behaviors and reinforcing them, because you are now aware of what you do want!

For instance, your dog is rearranging the furniture in nightly "puppy zoomics." Your dog runs around and around, completely out of control, sliding into furniture and knocking over lamps. Reinforce him when he's lying down being quiet and ignore the zoomies. As long as he's getting proper exercise, he'll lie down more often as a result.

The Art
If you know the time of day that he's going to race around the house, why not be pro-active and exercise him about 15 minutes before?

Many of the annoying behaviors your dog has can be easily changed and incorporated into your training. Turn an irritating behavior into an outlet for some exercise, or a reinforcer for good behavior.

When my own dog Beau was a puppy he used to steal my shoes and eat them. Rather than do the sensible thing and put my shoes away, I decided to teach him to retrieve them. As he paraded past me with a "neener, neener, neener" look on his face, I clicked and praised him. He dropped the shoe in surprise. I gave him a few treats and encouraged him to bring me the shoe. After repeating this a few times, he actually stopped stealing my shoes and brought me toys instead.

Even if your dog ends up always stealing things and bringing them to you for a treat, it's better than taking those same objects, eating them, and ending up in the emergency vet's office for surgery. The "two toy" game is discussed in Ch 11.

Ignoring What You Don't Like

Easier said than done. Now that you know what you do want, I'm sure you know what you don't want. You can address the unwanted behaviors in a few ways:

Completely and utterly ignore them—simply walk away, go into another room, or leave the house.

Redirect the dog to a desirable behavior, so you can then positively reinforce. Manage the situation better. For example, put your dog in his crate before he starts driving you crazy.

> ### Stipulations
> When you're redirecting the dog to a better behavior, be careful. You don't want to accidentally reinforce the dog for doing the "bad" behavior. For instance, you're busy and can't pay attention to your dog, so he then nips you or bothers you in inappropriate ways. You then redirect to a toy. What has your dog learned? "Bother Mom and Dad and they will play with me."
> This is how you should properly handle redirection: Dog is bothering you? Ask for an incompatible behavior—Sit or Down usually work well for most situations. Count to five while the dog remains in position. Then redirect the dog. This way, the dog associates "sit calmly and I get attention," rather than "be annoying and I get attention."

If you can't watch your dog because you're busy, simply put him in his crate beforehand with a nice juicy bone, and voilà! Instant Good Dog!

My motto is if you aren't ignoring the dog (for "bad" behavior), then you're reinforcing it. A student of mine was complaining that her dog was "dominant." I asked her what she meant by that. Her response, "He paws me all of the time." I asked, "So what is your response when he does that?" "I throw a toy." Okay! So her dog is doing something she doesn't want him to do, but inadvertently, she's reinforcing that unwanted behavior.

Breaking Down Each Behavior into Tiny Pieces (Approximations)

The key to training your dog is to help him experience success without the fear of making mistakes. This is achieved through approximation training. Picture a flip-book, where you flip the pages and it looks like a movie. Whatever behavior you want, make a mental flip-book of it. Then just train each page. The key to success is to know how to break each behavior down into its smallest components, step by step, so that your dog can understand the behavior. These small successes set him up to be right, thereby keeping his interest, as well as building his confidence.

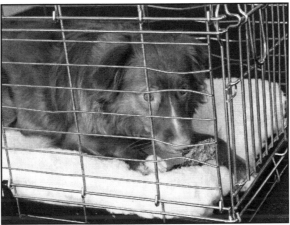

This dog is in her crate, happily chewing a bone.
Photo by T. Hirsch

The Art

Breaking behaviors into small segments, rather than lumping big chunks of behaviors together, makes it easier for the dog to understand. You didn't start out with calculus before you even knew that 1 + 1 = 2. Sometimes you need to get creative if your dog doesn't understand what you may think is a small enough approximation. And that in a nutshell is the "art" of dog training. Recognizing that your dog doesn't understand a behavior and breaking down a step into even smaller pieces. I've worked with some dogs that even a simple "sit" was way too complicated for them, so had to really put my thinking cap on and visualize the mechanics of how a dog sits and trained them that way.

> ### Definition
> Approximations are breaking behaviors down into small steps that when put together, make up a final behavior.

If you expect your dog to walk on a loose leash for a mile the first time you put a leash on him, you're setting him up to fail, and setting yourself up to be annoyed. Any behavior, no matter how seemingly easy (to you), must be broken down into very small steps for effective learning.

Keep Sessions Short and Successful

Continuous failure is a poor teacher. It can create a frustrated, aggressive or quitter animal — one that just hopelessly gives up. The optimal sessions are three to five minutes in length, three to five times per day, working on only two or three behaviors each time. If the behavior being taught is complicated, do even shorter sessions. Don't be afraid to train the dog for as little as 30 seconds or for just one correct repetition. A dog can see continual repetitions of behaviors (drilling) as a form of punishment. Even if the behavior is correct each time, it can get tedious. You want learning to be fun for your dog, not boring.

Fixing Bad Behaviors by Reinforcing Good Ones

Reinforce your dog for having four paws on the floor rather than jumping. Reinforce the dog for walking on a loose leash rather than pulling. Reinforce the dog for having a toy in his mouth rather than your arm. By focusing on the good, you'll be pleasantly surprised at how many times you actually get it!

My rule of thumb is this: if the dog does something great, reinforce within one-half to one second of the behavior. If the dog does something less than desirable, wait for a full five to ten seconds after he stops doing the unwanted behavior, redirect to a better one, and then reinforce.

The Positives of Modern Training

Positive training is easy on the dogs, it increases their love of learning, it gives them a better quality of life, facilitates communication and trust between owner and dog, and helps everyone lead happier lives.

On the other hand, positive training is hard on the trainer (at first) because you have to learn to use your brain (ouch!). It is much easier to yell, scold, spank, hit, and generally get angry, than it is to think, "What did I do to train my dog to act this way and what can I do to get him to stop?"

When our flawed human emotions come into play, our functioning brain cells disappear. It's hard to stop and reflect when we're emotionally charged. Once you're able to remain calm, training becomes easier and much more fun for you and your dog.

There's no magic answer to becoming more patient; it just takes practice and the sincere knowledge that losing your temper does nothing to help teach the dog anything. In fact, getting angry is more harmful than helpful—to both of you.

Modern training is extremely effective for teaching any species any behavior that they're physically capable of doing. You might say, "But how can not punishing my dog actually be more effective? I have to tell him what he did wrong."

The Art

A quote that may help you put it all into perspective: "Punishment is like a nuclear bomb. If the blast doesn't get you, the fallout will." -Steve White

Or let's compare punishment to drugs. You don't feel well and go to the Doctor and he/ she gives you a drug. It may suppress your symptoms, but suppression isn't a "cure." We all know that most drugs have side effects and now you have another symptom and have to go back to the Doctor for another drug to suppress that new problem. And so it continues. So yes, punishment may work, but the toxic fallout is unknown and therefore may be dangerous.

If you pay attention to only "good" behaviors, then your dog will continue to repeat what pleases you and what yields him your attention. If you pay attention to both "good" and "bad" behaviors, then you're confusing the heck out of your dog! Because both are being reinforced, then the dog will continue to do both.

The very idea that a dog "escapes punishment" or "gets away with it" is terrifying for some people. Our entire society is so punishment-based that it's hard for us to comprehend how an animal (or even a child) can actually learn better without it. But really, it works because attention is the best thing in the world to a dog (and humans, too). In fact, if you do physically or verbally punish the dog, you run a very high risk of creating much worse behaviors than the ones you started with.

Say that your teacher asks a question and you think you know the response. You raise your hand enthusiastically, blurt out your answer, and oops, you get it wrong. You get smacked for guessing incorrectly. The next time a question is asked you'll sit on your hands and avert your eyes to avoid the possibility of being called on. The rest of the class who witnessed your punishment will also be sitting on their hands.

> **Details**
>
> Leanne wanted to teach her dog Toby to lie down on his bed while she was eating dinner, instead of pestering her relentlessly and incessantly begging for food. Using the clicker and a small handful of treats, we taught Toby, in less than five minutes, to go to his bed when Leanne was eating.

Now for the flip side. The teacher walks in with a huge jar of candy and announces that anyone who attempts to answer a question will get a piece of candy. The students who give correct answers will get a whole handful of candy. More students will try harder, pay closer attention to the lesson, and do their homework more thoroughly and with more enjoyment. This system—positive reinforcement—encourages the students to think! It's more effective to teach dogs' minds rather than manipulate their bodies. Work with, rather than against, your dog during training sessions. Help inexperienced dogs rather than reprimand them.

Positively trained dogs—those who are not punished in the typical manner, will freely offer behaviors in an effort to elicit a good response from their trainers, grasp information more quickly, and often learn more advanced behaviors at a much earlier age than with most other training methods.

There are still some trainers out there who believe that dogs should work because they love us and we should not have to "bribe" them with food. I believe that while there may be some dogs somewhere who do things because they "love" us, it's rare. Eventually, if you build a strong relationship with your dog, he will someday just want to work out of the sheer joy of doing things with you. I don't believe in bribing a dog—I believe in reinforcing a dog for correct behavior—a paycheck, if you will. After all, most of us don't work for free unless we're independently wealthy. Behaviors that take months or years when using punishment-based methods are now taking weeks, days, hours, or even minutes to teach using positive methods.

The true spirit of positive-based training is the trust that the dog learns during the process.

The trust that he can offer behaviors without fear of recrimination. The trust that says you will not hurt your dog. We owe it to our dogs to keep that trust.

Pop Quiz

1. How many times did you notice that you used the word "no" with your dog today?

2. How many times did you catch your dog doing something right?

3. Did you reinforce for that "good" behavior?

4. How many times did you inadvertently reinforce your dog for doing something "bad"? (Reinforcements include yelling, saying "no," talking to the dog, comforting the dog, etc.)

5. Have you made the list of the behaviors you'd rather have your dog do?

6. What is an approximation?

Breaking down behaviors into tiny pieces

Summary

The fundamentals of positive training include reinforcing good behavior, ignoring bad behavior, breaking down desired behaviors into small steps, and watching your timing.

Be clear in your mind about exactly what behaviors you want from your dog.

Redirect your dog, or better yet, stop "bad" behaviors before they start.

Positive training is easy, and very effective. It is faster, has no bad side effects, and helps you and your dog have a happier relationship.

The laws of learning, like gravity, are always in effect.

BEHAVIOURS I WOULD RATHER HAVE MY DOGS DO.

- FEET ON THE FLOOR FOR VISITORS
- WALKING WITHOUT PULLING
- NOT BARKING IN THE CAR
- BE NICE TO OTHER DOGS
- COMING WHEN CALLED
- LEAVING THINGS WHEN ASKED TO
- BRINGING THINGS TO ME
- IGNORE HORSES GOING PAST
- STILL FOR GROOMING

10 Myths of Positive Training Dispelled 2

Why do myths, such as the ones that follow, spring up out of nowhere? Primarily due to the general lack of understanding of how classical and operant conditioning work, and its use in modern training. Here are my favorite responses to these misconceptions. It's hard to change old habits and old mind-sets; however, you'll see that modern training isn't so difficult after all. Going against the "old school" way may be difficult at times, but will be worth it in the end when you achieve a wonderful relationship with your well-mannered dog.

Myth #1: The Clicker Is a Fad or Gimmick

Marker training has been used for many decades with marine mammals, wild life and exotic animals as well as by competition and pet dog trainers. It is not new, and certainly not a fad. Using conditioned reinforcers (such as a clicker) is a training method based on sound, scientifically proven psychological principles, as discussed in Chapter 1. Skinner and others have conducted extensive research on the effectiveness of conditioned reinforcers in training with stable, unwavering results.

As with anything, if you use the clicker or positive training improperly, it won't work. Put your car into neutral gear and it won't move forward when you step on the gas pedal. Give your dog a treat for barking, "to shut him up," and he'll continue to bark.

I've seen ill-informed trainers use the clicker as a recall signal, as a sound with no meaning (in other words, no reward follows the sound), or just randomly, with no thought of what they were actually reinforcing. Use it incorrectly (marking the wrong behavior) and you can easily create confusion, fear, and avoidance.

Myth #2: The Principles Are Too Difficult to Learn and to Understand

This is absolutely not true. Although positive training involves a great deal of technical information, you don't have to be thoroughly versed or enmeshed to understand how it all works.

However, be warned that it's easy to become a "behavior junkie," because learning how dogs learn is fascinating. Many people come to me saying, "I just want a dog that doesn't jump or pull," and then become so mesmerized by the process that they stay to learn more.

Once you know the "whys" of behavior, it's then quite easy to fix problems—and better yet, stop them before they start.

Additional fallacies you may hear from tradition-based trainers:

> **Alert!**
> Without understanding at least some of the science behind the method I teach, it's easy to fall back into the punishment mode of training, especially when frustrated by your dog's behavior or perceived lack of progress.

Myth #3: Positive Reinforcement Takes Too Long

Actually, positive methods have been proven to speed up learning. In the beginning stages, it seems to take longer only because you may have to wait a whole five or ten seconds (!) for the dog to think, rather than forcing the dog into position.

However, once you and your dog catch on, modern training leads to faster results. Why? Creating an environment where the dog feels safe enough to learn and yes, maybe make a mistake along the way, is the cornerstone of modern dog training. Dogs quickly learn to perform desired behaviors in order to make you click so they can get paid! In this age of more things to do in less time, "faster" is a real asset. However, when building a relationship, it takes as long as it takes. You can't rush a bond—with dogs or with other people. In addition, behaviors learned through positive reinforcement and positive associations tend to be lifelong. You certainly can't build rapport and trust using punishment.

We all make choices in our lives. Sometimes we choose incorrectly. That is called a mistake. Dogs and people trained using positive methods sometimes make the wrong choices, as do dogs and people trained using punishment methods. At times, we all make the wrong choices—humans and dogs—because none of us is perfect. Did you get beaten the last time you goofed? If your dog makes a mistake, lighten up!

Many years ago I had a student that came to me with her adorable puppy and a very bratty 10-year old son. He was obnoxious toward his mother as well as to me. While he was taking the pup for a potty walk, I asked the mom what was up with her son. She explained that there was a great age difference between this boy and the next oldest sibling and that he was acting this way for attention.

I recommended that she treat him just as she would her puppy. If he was obnoxious, she was to turn around and leave the room. If he was appropriate, she was to reinforce him in any way that made sense to a 10-year old boy. The following week, he was a model of decorum, and it turned out he was really very bright and nice. During a break, when he was out of the room, I asked her, "Wow! What a difference! What did you do?" Her reply, "I did exactly what you told me to do and he is now correcting himself and apologizes if he forgets and talks back."

So in just one week of using positive methods, she was able to teach her son to behave properly, when for the last ten years, all the yelling yielded were impolite behaviors.

Myth #4: In Training, a Dog Should Never Be Given a Choice

Clicker trainers set up the situation so that their dogs make the desired choices. Dogs always have behavioral choices, even when they're trained with aversive consequences (corrections and/or punishment). To think they don't is an illusion.

I've seen dogs make mistakes regardless of whether they're trained using punishment or positive reinforcement. I've also seen people make mistakes—sometimes the same ones over and over again.

And if they do make a mistake — so what? No one is perfect!

Myth #5: You Must Always Have the Clicker with You

Although most modern trainers would probably admit to having clickers stashed everywhere (I personally found 15 clickers in my pocketbook the last time I cleaned it out), they're not necessary every time you work with your dog.

The clicker is used mostly when teaching a new behavior in the beginning stages. You can phase it out once the behavior is well learned. Thus, it is very important to make sure that certain words become secondary reinforcers. (A secondary reinforcer is something that the dog has to be taught to like) I use the words "yes" and "that's right" as my "click words." Sometimes it just isn't logical or practical to be holding food, clicker, toys, and the leash. Use these words not as praise, but as a marker signal followed by a reward, just as you would reward after a click.

Myth #6: Clicker-Trained Dogs Won't Work Without Food

I could counter that by saying that punishment-trained dogs won't work without punishment—like the above, it's just not true. In the beginning stages of training, I recommend that you use food liberally. Many times, the dogs have no real positive connection with training or their owners, and food helps to jump-start those connections. However, a good positive/clicker trainer learns how to go from continuous to variable schedules of reinforcement and to use other types of reinforcers, such as play, praise or toys. If you're still using the clicker, then the behavior isn't learned enough yet to phase it out. And that's okay — all things in due time!

> ### Definition
> If you give your dog a treat each and every time he does a correct behavior, you're following a continuous schedule of reinforcement. If sometimes you give the dog a treat for a correct behavior and sometimes you don't, then you're following a variable schedule of reinforcement. This is also often referred to as "the slot machine" effect—in other words, you never know when the payout will happen!

Food is sometimes easier to deliver and doesn't take much thought—get a behavior right, get a cookie. But if you use only food as reinforcement, the naysayers will be right—your dog will work only for food. Using other types of reinforcers, such as petting, play, or silly games, takes more thought and planning, but the benefits are enormous (see Chapter 12).

> ***Details***
> I used to be quite lazy about using reinforcers other than food. One of my dogs was consistently getting non-qualifying scores in competition obedience. I sat back and thought very hard about my training. Aha! The instant I started using toys, all kinds of play, and even silly pet tricks as reinforcers, he started not only qualifying, but getting very high scores as well.

Myth #7: Force Works Better

Although a dog's desire to avoid pain is strong, the desire to gain pleasant consequences is stronger. Think about the last time you got a speeding ticket—did it stop you from speeding? Much of your dog's behavior is based on what's more reinforcing for him do to.

Let's say you're stopped by the police each time you're not speeding and are rewarded with $100. Every day for a week, you're stopped two or three times per day and handed $100. Then the police go to a random schedule of reinforcement. Now you get stopped only one or two times per day and only three or five times per week. Sometimes you get verbally praised, sometimes you're handed dinner tickets to your favorite restaurant, and sometimes you get the $100.

Once in a while you get pulled over and handed $1,000. Would you ever speed again? I sure wouldn't. I would take that money and run out and buy a van with cruise control because I wouldn't want to miss out on being reinforcd so I can buy myself a new van! In the same respect, once a dog has learned something (good or bad), he tends to repeat that behavior over and over. Behaviors learned through force tend to fall apart when the dog is under stress. But behaviors learned in pleasant circumstances with positive consequences are less likely to fail under pressure.

Myth #8: Positive Training Isn't Effective with Barking or Aggression

Dogs trained using a clicker can be easily taught alternate behaviors to replace the unwanted ones. Trainers using positive principles often devise very creative ways to change undesirable behaviors such as barking and aggression. I've personally used positive training to solve a number of serious behavioral and aggression problems.

I've seen dogs barking in crates. I've seen their owners come up to the crate, kick it, yell at the dog, take the dog out of the crate when they can't stand it anymore or it becomes embarrassing, and otherwise reinforce the dog for barking in the crate.

I've seen owners put collars on their dogs that deliver an electric shock or a spray of citronella to get them to stop barking. After a few zaps with the shock collar or some sprays with the citronella collar, they hang the collar on the crate and say, "See? The dog is now not barking." True, but take the collar away and the dog starts barking again because now the threat of punishment is no longer there. And the dog hasn't learned anything constructive, such as being quiet in the crate.

Aggression can often be easily (although not necessarily quickly) corrected by using positive methods. You can't answer aggression with aggression and expect the dog to become friendly. Doing that would be the same as if someone was yelling or hitting you because you were afraid, and then expected you to go out and be the life of the party.

Myth #9: You Must Be Dominant to Your Dog

There are still arguments going on in the dog training world about the word and intent of "dominance." There are almost as many definitions of it as there are dog trainers. Yes, there are "dominant" dogs, just as there are "dominant" people. I think the real problem is that in our society we tend to think of the word "dominant" as being punitive, violent, scheming and coercive.

I feel the use of the word dominant clouds our perception of how to train dogs. What we are really trying to accomplish is compassionate leadership. Leadership between humans and dogs is about boundaries and acceptable behaviors for dogs living with humans. Adding compassionate understanding in training clarifies the roles in our relationship. The human, as leader, guides the dog, sets boundaries and teaches what is acceptable—with compassion—for the dog's long term well-being.

The behaviors we feel we cannot live with are usually natural canine behaviors; such as marking of territory, jumping on those they're happy to see, extensive barking to announce intruders. These behaviors are not attempts to subvert our leadership or organize a "coup." Really. Your dog isn't laying awake all night scheming how to take over your shared small world. Qualifying those behaviors as "dominant" is a misuse of the word and leads humans to believe there is intent from the dog where none exists.

I already stated in Chapter One that "positive doesn't equal permissiveness," and that "I never use physical or verbal punishment on my dogs. I don't rule by force and my dogs don't rule the roost." Being a leader for your dog is really about showing them the ropes, teaching them the rules—with compassion and being consistent with your expectations and cues.

I am sure you have experienced the following scenario; you ask your dog to do something, such as heeling and he completely blows you off. And yet when your instructor takes the leash and has a few treats, your dog acts like he has been trained for the Crufts Obedience Invitational. You get your dog back and he goes right back to ignoring you. Your dog isn't stubborn, stupid or acting "dominant" over you. Your instructor probably has a clearer picture in her mind of what she wants the dog to do, is very clear in her cues, and your dog is reading, understanding and complying.

Dominance has been attributed to many dog behaviors, most of which actually indicate an untrained or stressed dog, not a dominant one. Licking, jumping up in greeting, pulling on the leash, getting up on the couch, a dog with separation anxiety that destroys the house in his terror of being left alone, peeing in the house, ripping up pillows, going out of doorways first, sitting on your foot, nudging your hand for petting, barking, biting the leash, and the list can go on and on. I know a woman who was told (by her vet of all people!) that when she came home from work and her dog started licking his legs (creating lick granulomas) that he was acting dominantly toward her. None of these behaviors are about your dog showing "dominance" over you; they are all indicative of either an untrained dog or stress behaviors, and sometimes both.

Myth #10: TV shows are real life

Lately there are a ton of "reality" shows on TV about dog training. Please just remember that television is all about entertainment, (and ratings and money from advertisers) and have little to do with reality. Just like the police, lawyer and doctor shows, they all have little to do with real life or consequences. You wouldn't go into a courtroom thinking you have learned all you need to know about the law from *Law and Order* or perform surgery because you watch *House*.

No one can train a dog or solve serious behavioral problems in 30 minutes—it's just not possible. TV shows rarely have follow-up episodes to see how the so-called "cured" dogs are faring. An enormous amount of editing is involved, crucial information left unsaid and unaddressed and time lapses aren't shown. If your dog is having behavioral problems, please seek out a professional trainer, making sure you check references and certifications first.

Pop Quiz

1. If your dog is barking incessantly and you yell at the dog, what is your dog learning to do?

2. If your dog jumps on someone and you yank him down by the collar, what is your dog really learning?

Summary

Positive training is based on proven scientific principles.

Positive training does not take longer than punishment based training, and is in fact, often faster and more effective

Dogs always have choices in how they behave, regardless of the consequences and the training method.

Positive training is the only reliable way to deal with aggression.

Are You Listening to What Your Dog is Telling You? 3

Dogs are social animals, and a group of dogs is called a pack. No matter what the species, it's important for animals who live in large groups to have ritualized methods for avoiding aggression and conflict. Every species on this planet owns its own set of rules and regulations. Dogs give out approximately 50 signals that we humans can perceive. There are 12 signals we give to dogs that they may view as aggressive or threatening, according to their frame of reference.

This chapter is about communication. It explains the signals your dog is trying to give you and it also teaches you what signals you might be sending back without realizing it. With that understanding, you can learn ways to communicate, using your dog's own language.

The Art
Learning to read your dog is an art because there isn't a dictionary with every possible combination of signals defined. It will take some time, but once you "get it," you'll have a better understanding of your dog, as well as greater appreciation and trust.

Turid Rugaas, a Norwegian dog trainer, coined the words "calming signals" to describe how dogs communicate. Please see the Reading List in the Appendix for her book and DVD.

Why Dogs Give Off Calming Signals
We all possess ways of emitting certain signs or precursors that signify "I won't hurt you; I am a nice dog/person." Aggression must be inhibited, otherwise the pack will not survive. If there were no stopgaps, we'd all just kill each other and die out as a species.

In this country, making direct eye contact and reaching out to shake hands are seen as proper greeting behaviors. If someone refused to look at you or shake your hand, you'd feel uncomfortable or possibly suspicious. In other countries, direct eye

Definition
A precursor is a sign that something is going to happen. This can be a signal that the dog is getting nervous or a sign that something good is going to happen. An example of something good is the rattle of a plastic bag, signifying that a treat is coming.

contact and shaking hands can be perceived as a threat or the height of bad manners. While dogs do present some threatening signals—growling, barking, lunging, teeth baring—they show even more gestures to avoid conflict. Just as people from different cultures don't always understand each other's manners, people have trouble interpreting the signals that dogs exhibit. Dogs do in fact have a language, and I promise you, it isn't English. We must put dogs and their behaviors into perspective.

- Dogs behave like dogs because they're not fuzzy kids with four legs.

- Most humans don't understand dog behavior, because we're not naked dogs with only two legs.

- Dogs misinterpret our behavior and we misinterpret their behavior.

Understanding Your Dog's Signals

Get rid of any notion that your dog feels guilt, shame, and the like. Why? Because dogs are dogs! These are human emotions and dogs are a different species. However, dogs do have a very strict system of manners with fitting responses.

We humans are, for the most part, clueless regarding these behavioral responses because we're not dogs. The inability to communicate effectively with dogs is the overwhelming cause for almost every canine "behavior" problem. It's really a human problem, not a dog problem.

Dog communication is accomplished through a series of complex sounds, facial and body movements, and scents. The combination changes all of the time and the meanings are different each time. If the first sequence of signs is ignored, they

Child nicely keeping her hands to herself and not looking at the dog,
while the dog sniffs her.
Photo: Amy Locke

will try again, but with an increase in intensity and "bigger" signals.

> ### Details
> Marshall brought his seven-year-old Boxer, Brandy, to see me. Brandy had been nipping Marshall's one-year-old son in the face. Marshall loved his dog and was determined to fix this problem. By teaching Marshall the dog's signals, he was able to move his son away from the dog before the signals escalated. Within three weeks, the dog had completely stopped bothering the little boy. But more importantly, the little boy had stopped bothering the dog.

For instance, a child or adult is doing something that the dog regards as threatening. The dog may signal, nonverbally at first, that he's not happy with the behavior toward him. The adult or child doesn't notice and continues to pressure the dog.

The dog may use additional nonverbal signals and is ignored again. And again. The dog's signals may now include some verbal noises, such as a low growl. If the warnings are continually ignored, and the dog has been unable to make his point politely (within his own frame of reference), the signals will escalate into lifting his lip, snarling, showing teeth, snapping or biting.

> ### Details
> Lisa was volunteering in a shelter for homeless dogs. Shelters are very stressful places, and she wanted to help reduce their stress. After learning to recognize these signals, she utilized them during her visits. Within a few days, the dogs in the kennels were barking less, calming down faster, and able to focus better during the training sessions.

These types of behaviors that seemingly came "out of nowhere" didn't come out of nowhere at all—you just weren't paying attention.

The Art
I look at it this way: most dogs will communicate in whispers to start — small signals — a tiny lip lick, small head duck or head turn, a blink. If those are ignored or punished, they will have no choice but to "talk" louder by using more obvious signals — full sniffing, full body turns, huge yawns. If those are ignored or punished, they will start "yelling" and use even more blatantly (to them) obvious signals — frantic tail wagging, hackles up, low growl, showing teeth, stiffening of their body, staring. If those are ignored or punished, you may be leaving them no choice but to go further into conflict resolution with biting — into "poker face" mode and they will just simply bite with "no warning." The moral? Listen to and respect the whispers!

Is Your Dog Stressed?
As we know, life in general is stressful. Some stress is good and some can be devastating—both mentally and physically. Teaching your dog to accept a certain amount of anxiety is vital in creating a happy and healthy dog who will bounce back

quickly from everyday stressful events. The more common causes of stress are listed below. Some of them we can forestall and prevent; some we can't.

Stressed-Out Puppies

Here are some possible causes of stress for puppies:

- Stressed mother

- Born into a puppy mill including being taken away from mom and siblings too soon, transportation to, arrival and life at the pet shop

Dog doing a full mouth yawn and squinting his eyes
Photo: S. Staino

- Extensive travel

- Environment change (even when you get the dog from a reputable breeder)

- Tail docking, ear cropping, dewclaw removal

- Isolation or lack of proper food, water, or social contact

- Socializing the dog improperly or not at all

Stress for Adult Dogs

Here are some causes of stress for adult dogs:

- Moving, being given up for adoption, dumped, or abandoned

- Suddenly taking the dog to new places without training him to accept distractions in a variety of situations

- Not having been socialized as a puppy

- Sickness

- Too little or too much exercise

- Punishment

- Grooming and vet visits without proper desensitization beforehand

- Dissension in pack (human or canine)

- Being "corrected" (a politically correct word for punishment)

- Inconsistency in training

- Bitches coming into heat—stressful for both the bitch and any males who are around

A Brand-New Language: What the 50 Dog Signals Are

The following are 50+ perceptible (to humans) calming signals that dogs show. I've separated them into two columns — calming and stress. However, the line is often blurry between the two — not for the dogs of course, but for our own human understanding.

A list of the calming or stress signals that humans can observe in any dog:

Calming	Stress
• head turning away	• panting
• eyes turning away	• growling
• yawning	• spinning/circling
• sniffing	• stopped or frozen (in an awkward position)
• drooling	• howling
• lip licking	• short attention span
• raising a paw (as if to "shake")	• biting the leash
• grass eating	• poop eating
• marking	• whining
• excessive water drinking	• barking
• pooping	• aggression
• avoidance	• hyperactivity
• slow, reluctant behaviors	• complete body turns away from you (can also be calming)
• lowered body	• hackles raised
• hackles raised	• body shaking (as if they are cold)
• arcing (or curving)	• scratching
• laying down	• shaking (as if they were shaking off water)
• frantically wagging tail	• blinking of the eyes
• play bow	• sneezing
• splitting	• sweaty paws
• sitting	• raised temperature (ears can get hot)
• blinking	• diarrhea
• chewing	• "stress" shedding and dandruff
• squinting	• digging
• head lowered	• loss of appetite (won't take treats)
• slow movements	• frantically wagging tail
	• showing teeth

Big tongue lick.
Photo: S. Staino

Big tongue lick with a yawn, along with a head turn.
Photo: Amy Locke

"Mouth games." Both dogs on their backs, biting each others mouth and face. Great play!
Photo: S. Staino

Looks like a play bow — it isn't. Dog on right has a slight wall eye, is stiff and may be
starting to guard the ball.
Photo: S. Staino

More "mouth games." Perfectly normal play
Photo: S. Staino

More "mouth games." This time with slight rearing up, very wide mouths, but soft eyes and virtually no teeth showing, tail relatively soft.
Photo: S. Staino

More "mouth games." Teeth showing, but still play.
Photo: S. Staino

Dog in foreground is nervous — he's scratching
Photo: S. Staino

*Dogs playing nicely even though dog on top is gently biting the dog on the bottom
(no signs of stress from dog on bottom)*
photo: S. Staino

Definition
When dogs approach each other and wish to avoid fights, they arc around each other, like a capital C, rather than approach head on. They will arc in a big circle, at times even curving their bodies. This can calm the other dog and avoid a potential conflict.

*Might be enticing, but in this case, the dog's head is over the shoulder of the other dog and
he's leaning forward. Other dog's tail is slightly arced.*
Photo: S. Staino

Enticing play behavior — top of head under chin

Photo: S. Staino

Quite a bit going on in this photo. From left to right; Dog is nervous — head is lowered and you can see it by his facial expression. The next dog isn't quite arced away, but his tail is arced even though is body isn't (yet). Dog pouncing and pushing the next dog in line down with his foot. Dog being pushed down seems to be okay with it.

Photo: Amy Locke

Definition

When one dog runs between two other dogs who are playing rough, it's called splitting. He splits from the rear for obvious reasons (there are no teeth in the rear). Dogs often split up humans, too. This isn't jealousy; it's the dog's perception that the closeness is dangerous. Hackles are the hair along the spine or neck. The dog's hackles rise up when he is nervous or aroused.

These two dogs are both are a bit nervous. They are leaning slightly away from each other. Dog in background may be starting to lift a paw.

Photo: S. Staino

Submissive down, but in play. Both dogs have mouths open and tongues lolling. Dog on bottom does have an "agnostic pucker" — you can see the wrinkles on his snout. Dog on top— eyes relaxed, mouth soft. Based on the other body language both dogs are displaying, I'm not expecting a fight to ensue.

Photo: S. Staino

*Offering a submissive down. Tail tucked. Approaching from
below. I'm sensing the dog is nervous.*

Photo: S. Staino

*These two dogs are a bit unsure of each other. Dog in foreground has ears way back, mouth
is very tight. Dog in background is less nervous — glancing at other dog, soft ears, soft face,
but with a slight walleye.*

Photo: S. Staino

Nice dog play — soft body from dog on top, dog's face is alert but not intense. Body arcing, open mouth. A little hard to see the dog's face on the bottom, but face looks soft, ears relaxed, head not turned away.

Photo: S. Staino

Ambiguous Signals

Many of the calming signals listed are natural, normal behaviors, so you have to look at the context in which the dog is doing those things. If the dog has just finished playing or if it's a hot day, drinking would be a normal behavior. If, however, there is another dog around who is pestering your dog, water drinking would be a sign that he's nervous. Dogs will often keep drinking while looking at the other dog(s) and will stop drinking once everyone has calmed down.

A play bow can be an invitation to play, or it can be a sign of nervousness. I always look at the other dog to see what the play bow really means. If the other dog then plays, the bow was intended to entice. If the other dog goes off sniffing or engages in other behaviors, the bow was presented as an "I am nervous" signal.

I've seen peeing used as a distance seeking behavior — one dog will posture and another dog will back off.
Yawning and lip licking can also have two meanings. They can be natural—the dog is tired and yawns, or he's drawing in scent by licking. Or they can be signs of stress.

Each signal can be very subtle or it can be huge, depending on the situation. Yawning can be a slight opening of the mouth, or wider with a little tongue curl or huge with a big tongue curl, huge with a little bit of teeth showing or huge with all of the teeth showing. Again, when looking at yawning or lip licking, take into consideration the context of the situation.

Dog in the middle is splitting up too rough play.

Photo: P. Dennison

Big tongue lick, head lowered and eyes squinting.

Photo: S. Staino

Dog on right and on left are both showing their weapons (teeth) about the same amount. However, the dog on the right is also slightly sticking out his tongue, which is the white flag saying, "can we please stop now?" The dog in the background on the right with the huge mouth open, is just barking.

Photo: K. Chittenden

Personal Stress Signals

In addition, there are also what I call "personal" stress signals. To recognize these, it is imperative that you really examine and learn the individual look of your dog when happy and at rest. These personal stress signals are different for every dog and can involve any of the following:

- The set of the ears and tail

- Any creases on the face

- The outline of the nose and muzzle, which can change when a dog feels stressed

- The look and shape of the eyes and pupils

- Foaming or bubbling at the mouth (different than drooling)

- Tightness of his mouth or hesitancy when taking food

- Suppleness or tightness of his body and face

- Puffing out of cheeks with short but explosive breaths

Submissive down, dog on top is also showing some calming signals — paw lifted, not looking directly at dog on the bottom.

Photo: S. Staino

Looks like a play bow, but hackles are slightly up on dog in foreground who is clearly bark-ing at the Boxer. Boxer's ears are back and his front end is leaning a bit away and his hind end is closer to the other dog (he's almost in an arc) as an appeasement or perhaps a play behavior. Boxer does have a small bone in his mouth, so the other dog may be trying to get it or may be trying to just play.

Photo: S. Staino

Sniffing rear ends. You can clearly see the arced body on the dog on the right.

Photo: P. Dennison

Every dog is unique. Some dogs have cropped ears or docked tails and so some of these signals don't apply. Some dogs show their nervousness by enlargement of their pupils, but in some dogs it's the complete opposite—their pupils get very tiny. Again, this is why it's important to learn your dog's language.

Dog on right is showing her weapons (teeth) and the dog on the left is leaning backwards.
Photo: T. Hirsh

Body Language That May Stress Your Dog

It's important to note that dogs are Canids and we are Primates. Dogs may annoy us with their normal greeting behaviors — jumping, licking, sniffing. We, on the other hand, employ a great deal of primate based behaviors using arms, hugging, hands reaching out and face. Many dogs find these threatening.

Actions that may cause stress to your dog:

• Leaning over the dog

• Forcing your face in the dog's face

• Petting the dog on the withers (shoulder blade) area

• Petting the dog around the face and especially on the top of the head

• Walking straight into the dog

• Eye contact (especially with a strange dog)

• Hands reaching down to the dog

These next five are rooted in misguided training. Please stay away from them.

- "Alpha" rolls

- Scruff shakes

- Hitting

- Yelling

- Forcing the dog into position (such as a "Sit" or "Down")

Can you teach your dogs to accept the first seven human signals without becoming fearful or aggressive? Of course you can, and you must. Although I'd prefer it if you didn't scare your dog while doing so. It is imperative to teach your dog to accept all types of obnoxious human behavior. If you don't, you're headed for some big problems. See Chapter 7 for teaching your dog to accept handling.

*Dog isn't happy with being hugged tightly —
tongue is sticking out.*

Photo: S. Staino

*Hand reaching out toward dog — dog's ears are
back, tongue is out and head is turned slightly away*

Photo: V. Wind

*Teaching the same dog to accept human faces and
hands coming toward his head.*

Photo: V. Wind

Ways That You Can Reduce Your Dog's Stress

Except for the more disgusting behaviors such as marking, poop eating, grass eating, and the like, we humans can communicate directly to our dogs using some of the same language they use. You can quite effectively use the following in most cases:

- Avert your eyes

- Avert your face

- Turn your back on the dog

- Walk slowly away

- Freeze in position (but be sure to breathe!)

- Yawn

- Lick your lips

- Sit

- Lie down

- Kneel on the ground and pluck grass

- Look down

- Turn sideways

- Blink

- Split in between another dog or person

- Arc or curve

- Walk parallel to the dog

Instead of forcing ourselves on dogs, we can use these signs to entice them to come to us. A typical greeting can be the following:

- Glance in the dog's direction and quickly avert your eyes, or even blink a few times.

- While looking away, lick your lips and/or yawn.

- Glance back again; then turn your head and body away from the dog.

- Move away slowly for a few steps.

- Squat or kneel down, turning your body sideways to the dog.

- Keep your hands to yourself. Let your arms drop naturally by your side and wait for the dog to approach.

If at any time the dog sniffs the ground, avoids you, yawns, or licks his lips, you may answer him back with some of your own signals. Be sure to discontinue your approach and just move away slowly. Never pressure a dog to say "hello" or force him to approach something that he's afraid of, as you'll only increase his fear and possibly make him worse.

By learning and practicing these simple signals, you can effectively learn to communicate with your dog. By always keeping an eye on your dog and heeding the multitude of signals he's giving you about his emotional state, you can avoid potential problems.

How Will Knowing Your Dog's Signals Help You Train Him?

I truly believe that 90% of what it takes to train a dog is to be able to read them properly and 10% is all of the dozens of verbs we can teach them. Trust and effective communication creates a back and forth "conversation" that not only enhances your relationship but also speeds up the learning process.

If your dog is stressed and you don't know it, you might mistakenly believe that you have a stupid or stubborn dog. He may be nervous about a new location or new people, but you believe that he's being "bad" when he ignores you because he's shut down due to fear. So you end up jerking him around and in effect, punishing him for being afraid. We all know that's neither fair nor kind.

Learn to read your dog for signs of stress. If a child or stranger is approaching and your dog exhibits early signs of stress (lip licking, head turning, backing away, etc.), don't allow the person to approach any closer. Allowing them to continue to approach will either put the dog into a more defensive posture or cause him to be more afraid.

If your dog doesn't like petting on the head (by the way, 99 % of all dogs don't like it), then, until you condition him to accept it, don't pet him on the head. Think your dog does? Try this test: call him over to you and pet him on the head. If he avoids your touch, ducks his head, moves away completely, or moves his head toward your hand (as if to bite—even without a show of teeth), well, guess what? Your dog is part of the ninety—ninth percentile and is completely normal.

Growling

A growl is an important mode of communication. It's not necessarily aggression—it's a warning. When the police say, "Stop or I'll shoot," this doesn't mean that they will shoot regardless of what you do or don't do; it's a warning.

If you punish a dog for growling, you deny yourself the heads—up that your dog is feeling threatened. If you're smart, you'll thank your dog for growling because he's just letting you know that he's very uncomfortable, and if you don't stop what you're doing, he may bite. A growling dog doesn't want to bite you—that's why he's growling—it's a warning for you to stop what you're doing.

If the dog is growling at you, please, please, pretty please don't take it personally.

> ### Pointers
> I was working with a German Shepherd Dog a few years ago. I knew her as a puppy to be a wonderfully sweet dog. Two years later, the owner brought her back to help work with her aggression. I watched the dog move and I had this feeling that something was wrong with her hind end. She would bite you if you touched anything past her waist. I told the owner to take the dog to the vet. Turns out the dog had a broken tail!

Your dog is just telling you that he doesn't like whatever it is you're doing. There may be an underlying cause — physical or mental—for the growling. Perhaps you hurt him inadvertently or he has a boo—boo that you don't know about.
After making sure there's no hidden medical reason, use the growl as a wake—up

> ### Definition
> Desensitization or systematic desensitization is a form of counter-conditioning, a procedure in which a phobic (scared) subject (human or animal) is subjected to low levels of the frightening stimulus while relaxed. The level of frightening stimulus is gradually increased, but never at a rate to cause distress. Eventually, the fear dissipates.
>
> Counterconditioning is the use of classical conditioning to reverse the unwanted effects of prior conditioning.

> ### *Alert*
> When I was a groomer, one of my clients — a lovely, well-adjusted, happy Springer Spaniel, all of a sudden one day started growling at me, and his eyes were very scary. When his owners came to pick him up, I explained what had happened and asked about any changes in the household, diet, or health. They'd also noticed a slight change in the dog's behavior, and, upon further examination, learned that the new baby-sitter was abusing both the dog and their grandson.
>
> The moral? Don't ever punish your dog for growling—listen to what he's saying. I knew that the aggressive display was out of character. Because I didn't let it go, the dog and child were saved from a bad situation.

call to train the dog to accept whatever it is that made him unhappy. If you see these signs, you must desensitize and countercondition your dog to whatever it was that made him nervous.

Stopping Bad Behaviors in Stressful Situations

You can (and should) stop undesirable behaviors preferably before they start or escalate. To do that, you'll need to be aware of your dog's subtle signs of stress and quickly intervene on his behalf. Waiting until your dog is in full defense mode is counterproductive. Dogs in defense mode are highly aroused, their heart rate increases, and their adrenaline and glucocorticoid levels are high. For some dogs it can take between two to six days for these stress hormones to come down to normal levels. Until then, the dog's ability to learn is compromised.

> ### *Definition*
> Adrenaline and glucocorticoids are hormones produced in mammals during stress to help the body prepare for a fight-or-flight response.

Any added stressor that the dog comes into contact with before the hormone levels go back to normal will set the dog's stress clock even higher, and the dog may react even more vehemently.

Strangers

If you have a dog that is fearful or unsure of strangers and one is approaching full tilt to pet your dog, tell the other person to stop his or her approach, or simply walk

> ### *Pointers*
> Some people might insist on approaching your nervous dog, perhaps saying, "Oh, it's okay, I have dogs at home," or some other such nonsense. It's up to you to keep your dog safe from people like this. You wouldn't allow a stranger to approach and touch your child, would you? Of course not. So don't allow strangers to approach and handle your dog when they have no invitation to do so, especially if your dog has already shown that he's uncomfortable.
>
> I personally handle it this way — if someone approaches and stops at least 10-15 feet away and asks politely if they may pet my dogs, I reinforce their behavior by allowing it. If someone races up uninvited and tries to pet my dogs, I quickly move away and do not reinforce their inappropriate behavior; i.e.: I don't allow them, and as an added bonus, I give them my standard lecture on how dangerous it can be to race up to strange dogs.

away. The general public doesn't own your dog and there's no law that I know of that insists that the general public must be allowed to pet your dog. It is up to you as the owner to keep your dog safe and be mindful of his comfort levels in stressful situations.

There is some old wives' tale that says you must reach out a hand to let the dog sniff you, and after that, it's okay for you to pet him on the head. Like most old wives' tales, this is wrong! As we learned, the dog sees this as threatening. The proper thing to do is to crouch down to the dog's level, (from a distance) turn sideways, no eye contact, keep your hands to yourself and let him sniff you at his own pace. And just because he may sniff you, this is not an invitation for petting. Pushing their nose under your arm repeatedly — that's an invitation for petting! If the dog moves away then you know he's uncomfortable.

Leashes

Not every dog has to be friends with every other dog. My preference is that my dogs be calm around all other dogs, rather than expect playmates in all the dogs we see. After all, we don't like every person we meet either. And just because my dogs are friendly doesn't mean other dogs they meet are the same. Safety first!
You can inadvertently teach your dog to be aggressive by the way you use your

Dogs being allowed to greet on leash. Dog in center is clearly nervous and the dog in fore-ground is also tense and pulling forward.
Photo: A. Locke

leash. You should use the leash as a safety net, not as a tool. Your relationship is what should control the dog. Leashes and collars can break or be yanked out of your hand. If you use the leash as a tool, you really don't have a relationship with your dog.

If you continually yank on your dog, then you're stressing him and he can't concentrate on anything other than "You're hurting me! Stop it!" He then may redirect onto the next object he sees.

> *Definition*
> Redirect or redirected aggression means to take an emotion that a dog (or human) can't express in a situation or at an intended target, and direct it toward something else. For example, your boss just yelled at you, so to alleviate the stress you're feeling, you yell at anyone it is "safe" to yell at.

A dog on a tight leash, just by virtue of being confined, feels defensive—he can't escape danger and he knows it. That's why so many dogs are aggressive when they're on a leash. I personally never allow my dogs to greet other dogs on leash — ever. If I'm out on the trail and I see a loose dog coming, I drop my leash. My dogs can keep themselves safer and communicate better when they're not on leash. The obvious proviso would be if we were really being attacked, I'd pick them up.

If you yank your dog away from another dog, yell or become excitable yourself, the state of arousal in the dog becomes higher and higher until what perhaps started as a simple, "Hi, who are you, and what's your name?" can quickly become, "Come any closer and I'll rip your throat out!" If your dog doesn't yet walk on a loose leash around other dogs, avoid the company of other dogs until you've trained more. You can certainly do some off-leash work if the other dogs are friendly and the area is safe.

Set Up for Success

If you are aware of what causes your dog distress, then limit his access to the feared objects or situations, and slowly, methodically go in closer while reinforcing for calm behaviors. Until you can take the time to train your dog to accept the human world in all its complexities, manage the situations as best you can so that your dog doesn't practice nervous or fearful behaviors. After all, practice makes perfect, whether the behavior is "good" or "bad." Controlling your environment and encounters allows the dog to practice only what you like. If you need professional help, see the Appendix for references to positive dog trainer organizations.

What else can you do to ensure that your dog grows up with a healthy attitude in this complex and intricate world we live in? You can educate yourself, your family, and your friends about canine behavior and body language. Get your pup out and about as much as possible, from the time he's eight weeks old, always moving at his pace and his comfort level. Teach your dog manners and acceptance of the human species they now live with. Observe, watch over, and listen to your dog—in his language.

Homework

Read over this chapter a few times, and during the week, pick a few signals to watch out for, such as lip licking, head turning, and yawning. Then watch your dog(s) carefully and become "fluent" in those signals. Then next week, pick a few more signals. Continue to observe your dog, until you can really see the small subtleties of your dog's body language. You will find a whole new fascinating world has opened up for you and you'll have a greater understanding and appreciate of him.

Get Turid Rugaas' DVD and watch it at least a dozen times. Really!

Pop Quiz

1. Why is it a good idea not to punish your dog for growling?

2. Why do many dogs act differently when on leash versus when off leash?

3. Name a few ways you can calm your dog down if he's stressed.

4. If your dog doesn't like petting, what should you do?

5. If your dog is nervous and showing fear by either backing away or growling, what should you do?

Summary

Dogs give off "calming signals" to keep the peace.

We unknowingly do things that stress our dogs.

Be aware of your dog's signals to avoid potential problems.

Humans can use many signals that dog's use.

Watch your dog at all times for signs of stress or fear—and do not punish these signs.

Learn to manage your dog's stressful encounters.

Use your leash as a safety net, not as a tool.

The ABCs of Learning 4

As I touched on a little in Chapter 1, the basis of all learning (for both humans and dogs) happens within either classical conditioning or operant conditioning.

Learning is "a change in behavior due to experience." As teachers of our dogs, we need to make their experiences as pleasant as possible. We all know that behavior is influenced by its consequences. We reward or punish people and dogs so that they will behave in different ways.

The Basis of All Learning

There are three components to every learned behavior. Just remember your ABCs:

Antecedent: A cue, or something that comes before a behavior

Behavior: What the animal does, resulting from the cue

Consequence: What happens directly after the behavior

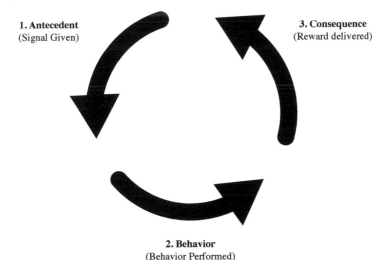

1. Antecedent
(Signal Given)

3. Consequence
(Reward delivered)

2. Behavior
(Behavior Performed)

This is the sequence in which operant conditioning happens. You can't have the behavior before the antecedent, and you can't have the consequence before the behavior.

A Is for Antecedent

An antecedent, more commonly called a "cue," is anything that happens before a behavior. We're surrounded daily by all kinds of antecedents, and we adjust our behavior accordingly. For a person, this can be a red traffic light, a lightning bolt, the alarm clock, the promise of a paycheck, the doorbell ringing, or Mom saying "Let's all go for ice cream." To a dog, antecedents can include such things as a person approaching, the sound of a can opener, or seeing the leash coming out. These are all antecedents that tell a person or a dog how to react next.

B Is for Behavior

The next step in your ABCs is "B," the behavior—or how you or your dog will respond to the antecedent. The red light tells you to stop, the lightning bolt tells you to run for cover, the alarm clock wakes you up, the promise of a paycheck

> *Pointers*
> Every event in our daily lives has an antecedent, behavior, and consequence. The antecedent can be a sign of something pleasant or something punishing to come.

inspires you to work, a doorbell ringing means answer the door, and "ice cream" is pretty obvious. To a dog, a person approaching could mean jump up and display submissive behavior, like licking and pawing at the person (unless you've trained him that a person approaching is a cue to sit). Hearing the can opener means run to the kitchen, and seeing the leash coming out of the closet means run to the door to go out.

C Is for Consequence

So what happens once you've seen the antecedent and done the behavior? Now comes the "C," the consequence. Stop at a red light and you won't get into an accident or get a ticket. Run for cover and you won't get struck by lightning. Wake up when the alarm rings and you won't be late for work. Pick up your paycheck and you get to go shopping and pay your bills. You open the door, Publisher's Clearing House is there, and you've won a million dollars (and now you don't have to set the alarm anymore to get up and go to work). Again, the ice cream is obvious.

The dog gets attention for jumping (or for sitting), he gets fed after the can is opened, and he goes for a walk after the leash is put on.

The behavior and consequence can also be something good or bad, and can change. For instance, if you allow your puppy to bite you when you're playing with him, here's how you've trained your dog:

- You get down on the floor (antecedent).

- The dog bites you for attention (behavior).

- You play with the dog (consequence).

Now the dog is older and you no longer want him to bite you, so here's what you can do:

- You get down on the floor (antecedent).

- The dog bites you with adult teeth and it hurts (behavior).

- You punish the dog by hitting or yelling at him, or you use the proper positive trainer response, which is to get up and leave (consequence).

> *Alert!*
> Please don't allow a puppy to do what you won't want him to do as an adult dog. It will only confuse and stress the dog, and annoy the heck out of you. Think ahead!

The Four Main Principles of Operant Conditioning

Positive reinforcement, negative reinforcement, positive punishment, and negative punishment are the main terms of operant conditioning, and these can be confusing at first. Although you may not need to know these terms to train your dog, I want you to be aware of them and how they do, in fact, relate to how quickly your dog learns, both the good and the bad.

In science, the terms "positive" and "negative" relate only to adding (positive) something or taking (negative) something away. The terms "reinforcement" and "punishment" relate to behavior increasing (reinforced) or decreasing (punished):

- **Positive Reinforcement (+R):** Anything that is added (positive) that increases (reinforces) behavior.

- **Positive Punishment (+P):** Anything that is added (positive) that decreases (punishes) behavior.

- **Negative Reinforcement (–R):** Anything that is taken away (negative) to increase (reinforce) behavior.

- **Negative Punishment (–P):** Anything that is taken away (negative) to decrease (punishes) behavior.

Now that you're thoroughly confused, the following sections give you some examples, to help you gain a better understanding of these concepts.

Positive Reinforcement

Here are some examples: your dog sits when you ask and you give him a treat; thus, his sitting behavior will increase in the future. You give your dog treats for walking on a loose leash, and his loose-leash-walking behavior will increase. You reinforce your dog for not rearranging the

furniture, and "lying down calmly" behaviors will increase. You reinforce your dog for having "four on the floor," and his staying-on-the-floor behavior will increase.

Positive Punishment

Don't be confused by this—positive means something added, but not necessarily something nice. You touch a hot stove and burn your hand. You will not touch a hot stove again. Your dog is barking and you turn on the citronella collar. His barking may decrease. Your dog urinates on the rug and you hit him with a newspaper, and his eliminating on the rug behavior may decrease.

I do not advocate positive punishment. In fact, I highly recommend that you stay away from it. There are too many toxic side effects. The timing has to be perfect (if you punish the dog for soiling the house after he comes to you, you have just punished him for coming to you), and punishment is usually associated with the person doling it out, not necessarily the undesired behavior.

Oftentimes, you only partially suppress behavior using positive punishment—sure, the dog stops urinating on the carpet, but now does it behind the couch. For some dogs, barking is so self-reinforcing (i.e., they like to bark) that they'll bark regardless of what you do, or bark only when the shock or citronella collar is off. The punishment has to outweigh the motivation and reward for it to be truly effective.

Depending on the motivation, some people (and dogs) will go to great lengths to succeed over adversity, un-relentlessly finding a way to continue their desired behaviors regardless of the punishment or hardships.

Remember: "Punishment is like a nuclear bomb; if the blast doesn't get you, the fallout will."

Negative Reinforcement

Negative reinforcement increases a behavior by taking something away that the dog doesn't like. Of course, you must have already added these punishers to be able to then take them away.

So what starts out as positive punishment can end up being negative reinforcement. The choke collar is yanked and then loosened up when the dog stops pulling. You hit the dog and then stop hitting him when he ceases to jump. The electricity is turned off, and then turned back on after you pay the bill. As with positive punishment—don't do it!

Negative Punishment

By the sound of it, this must be the most awful option. It isn't, though, and in fact is the method of choice that positive trainers use to "punish" their dogs. I did tell you that I do punish my dogs—and this is how I do it.

Historically, we humans are controlled primarily through negative reinforcement. We're punished when we haven't done what is reinforcing to those who are in "charge" (such as parents, employers, or trainers). Positive reinforcement has, unfortunately, been less often used, even though it is more effective than negative reinforcement and has many fewer unwanted by-products.

For example, a student is punished when he doesn't study. He may study after that, but, out of anger and frustration, he may also stay away from school (truancy), vandalize school property, attack teachers, or do nothing. With positive reinforcement, the student would have been reinforced for studying in the beginning of school year, and most likely would have learned to love learning and attending school.

Negative punishment reduces behaviors by taking away or withholding something good or something the dog will work for. Your dog jumps on you and you walk away, thus withholding the attention he craves. His jumping behavior will decrease.

Your dog is being pushy and demanding attention. You walk away, denying the dog your attention. The next time your dog will sit politely for attention, reducing the pushy behavior. You ask your dog to sit and he looks at you blankly. You withhold the treat. The next time you ask him to sit, he will sit, reducing the "looking at you blankly" behavior.

You're playing ball with your dog and he brings it back but won't drop it. You end the game. The next time you play ball, he will drop the ball, reducing the "hold on to the ball at all costs" behavior so as to enjoy more play. The bad do bad because the bad is rewarded. The good do good because the good is rewarded.

Classical Conditioning (Associative Learning)

Classical conditioning is an association between two stimuli. Of these two stimuli, one is neutral and in the beginning has no meaning. The other stimulus is one that does already have meaning for the dog (or human). The stimulus can be pleasant, or it can be unpleasant.

The two main events that humans or dogs don't need to learn to react to without training are food and pain. Almost everything else is a learned association.

Let's go back (just for a minute) to Pavlov, the metronome, the dog, and the saliva. When Pavlov first started pairing the sound of the metronome just before food was presented, the dogs did

> **Definition**
> Stimuli (the plural of stimulus) are any events that affect or are capable of affecting behavior.

not drool. However, over time, with consistent pairing (metronome and then food), the dogs began to salivate at the sound of the metronome. As far as their automatic reactions were concerned, the metronome meant food.

Why Is Classical Conditioning Used?

Classical conditioning is used for two reasons:

- To create an association between a stimulus that would not normally have any meaning along with a stimulus that would have meaning

- To train automatic responses (e.g., drooling, blinking, or even emotions can be considered automatic responses)

Of course, we don't really need to teach our dogs to blink or drool, but the emotion part is important to us. The recess bell has no meaning until it's paired with playtime; the word "Sit" has no meaning unless paired with sitting; and the smoke alarm has no meaning until you see the fire.

Classical conditioning is largely responsible for our reflexive motivation to respond in any situation. For example, we smell bread baking; we feel hungry and possibly even start salivating.

Operant behavior is voluntary behavior that is influenced by its consequences. We smell bread baking and get out a plate and some butter. Whether wanted behaviors occur in the future depend upon the nature of the consequence. If doing the behavior makes life better for the dog (or us, for that matter), it will most likely happen again in the future.

Your dog meets a person who gives him lots of yummy treats. The next time he meets that person, he'll be happy to see her. Associations, especially first ones, are vitally important to how a dog views his world. You can easily create a happy, well-adjusted dog or a fearful, aggressive dog by the associations you allow him to have.

Bad Associations

Setting up a dog to be fearful or aggressive is easy to do. Here's how: make sure all his associations are bad ones. For example, let your dog meet someone who will knee him in the chest or yell if he jumps. The next time he meets that person, your dog won't be happy to see him or her. Do this enough times and your dog will be fearful of people.

> ### Alert!
> Beware of "negative" associative learning. Your dog runs away and comes back an hour later. You punish him for running away—only, he understands it as punishment for returning. The next time you say "Come," he will stay away because that word was paired with unpleasant results.

Here are some other ways to set up bad associations: introduce your young puppy to an older dog who isn't good around puppies, and watch your dog grow fearful or aggressive toward strange dogs. Yell at your dog for a myriad of "bad" behaviors and he'll learn to either ignore you or be afraid of you. Call your dog to come and then punish him for something he did an hour ago; now the word "Come" takes on a negative connotation. Hit your dog for growling at a child and watch your dog learn to hate children (and probably progress from growling to biting). Punish your dog for making a mistake during training and he will then associate training with pain, which certainly does nothing to help him love learning.

Keeping Those Good Associations Happenin'

So what can you do? Make sure the life-experiences and associations are good ones! Have your puppy play with friendly dogs and meet nice, dog-friendly people. Use positive reinforcement as your training philosophy. Get rid of punishments from people, dogs, and (as much as possible) the environment. Yes, even the environment can be punishing. Inanimate objects can be dangerous! Lamps can fall, baby gates can get stuck on doggies' necks, doors can slam in faces, and paws can get stuck in crate doors. Honking horns and wailing sirens can send many a dog under the table in fear.

Pop Quiz

1. Define antecedent, behavior, and cue.

2. Can you come up with your own examples of positive reinforcement, positive punishment, negative reinforcement, and negative punishment?

Summary

All learned behaviors have an antecedent, a behavior, and a consequence.

Positive reinforcement creates the most reliable behaviors.

Negative punishment is the best way to punish your dog.

Foundation Skills 5

This chapter discusses the importance of building a relationship with your dog, and then teaching some basic skills. Without mutual attention and focus from both sides of the leash, training becomes very difficult if not impossible.

To get the behaviors you want and need from your dog, you must build a relationship first. In fact, 90 percent of all dog training is building your relationship and learning to read your dog (as discussed in Chapter 3). The other 10 percent is the actual obedience and manners. Try to get manners without the relationship and you won't succeed.

Don't think that the relationship is included in the purchase price of a puppy—you have to earn that over the course of years. Dogs do things that work for them. Does that make them selfish? I don't think so. We all do things that work for us. That's what makes us human and what makes them dogs.

Any fun or relaxing activity you share with your dog builds up some nice money in the bank account of your relationship, which in turn aids your training as well and enriches you both.

Just Say No to "No"

The first step is to stop all negativity. Drop all physical and verbal punishments, including the word "No." "No" very easily escalates into a screamed "No!" dredging up some very negative emotions from us, which is then transmitted to the dog. Remember—classical conditioning happens 24 hours a day, 7 days a week, whether you want it to or not. You just can't get away from Pavlov!

Look at it this way. Verbs are our friends! "No" is not a verb. No" doesn't tell the

> ### Details
> Positive training might very well change your life as well as your dog's. Sally and John brought their Golden Retriever pup for training. After six weeks of diligently practicing with their dog each week, they told me that they actually stopped saying "No" to each other! Another client, Henry, was a very sullen, negative person with job-related problems and two very nice mixed-breed puppies. After training with me for a few weeks, he mentioned that positively training his dogs had turned his life around. He started to treat his co-workers in a more positive manner and was doing a better job at work. The best part is that everyone on the job noticed and complimented him on his change of attitude. Positive reinforcement from positive change!

you want him to do instead of what he is doing at the moment. "No" does nothing positive for the relationship between you and your dog. Imagine living with someone who is always nitpicking, screaming at you, hitting you. After a while you may just give up because nothing you do is "right." It's the same with your dog; focus on what he's doing right and you'll all be happier.

You may hear the term "NRM" (no reward marker). This simply means using words that tell the animal he did something wrong and no reward is forthcoming. While on the surface it sounds like a good idea, it isn't. No matter how nicely you say it or what "soft" word you use, it's still a punishment.

> ***Pointers***
> There are four magic words to use instead of "No" — "Come," "Sit," "Stay," and "Give." Once your dog has learned what these behaviors mean, use them instead. If your dog has his paws up on the counter — "Come" works well. If your dog is digging through the garbage — "Come-Sit-Give" are the words you should use.

Words to stay away from are "Eh-eh," "Oops," "Wrong," "Phooey" — and any other words you come up with to mean "No." "No" is counter-productive, and you'll get better behaviors faster without it.

The Science
If your dog gets a behavior wrong, just pause for about 3-6 seconds and then resume. This is often called an LRS (Least Reinforcing Stimulus) or NCR (No Change Response). They both simply mean that you should do nothing that will either positively or negatively impact the dog.

There aren't really any "good" or "bad" behaviors — there are just behaviors. Good and bad are subjective. I allow my dogs on the furniture, so for me, getting on the furniture is a "good" behavior. Other people may dislike having their dogs on the furniture, so for them, getting on the furniture is a "bad" behavior.

Begin at the Beginning
Before any training can start, you need to make the click sound valuable and meaningful, and you need to teach him that eye contact with you, hearing his name and "Come," are worth a million bucks. Why? Because you cannot train a dog that isn't focused on you.

What is a Learned Behavior?
Many people mistakenly think that a dog who happens to perform a behavior once or twice on cue actually knows the cue. You may think that your dog is just being stubborn or stupid, but in reality he is just undertrained. Most dogs haven't experienced enough correct repetitions in enough varied situations to have a complete and deep understanding of the cue and the behavior expected of them.

Dogs are notoriously poor generalizers—just because your dog knows the behavior at home, does not mean that he will know it elsewhere. What your dog learns in the kitchen, stays in the kitchen!

The Science

I like to use behavioral psychology's definition of a learned behavior: "A learned behavior is one that occurs correctly in at least 8 out of 10 tries, out of 10 trials." If your dog cannot perform a behavior correctly 80 out of 100 times, then he hasn't learned it yet. It's that simple. I would like to add my own addendum to that definition—"and in at least 15 new and different locations with varying degrees of distractions." If this sounds daunting, take heart! The more novel environments and distractions you add in, the quicker your dog will learn to generalize.

First Things First

I'd like you to know that clicker training isn't 100% related to the actual clicker. It's about using a marker signal (any signal) to tell your dog that he did something right.

The Art

It's also about changing your own mindset - from looking at what your dog is doing wrong, to recognizing when they're right. From taking that positive mindset and instead of negatively impacting your dog, to training different and more appropriate behaviors. The actual clicker is not something you'll use forever and it's not a magic wand.

First of all, start your session by priming the clicker to teach your dog that "click" means food. Count out 60 treats. Put your arms down by your sides. Your dog will be in front of you and follow these steps:

1. Click the clicker.

2. Hand your dog one treat within a half second after the click (this is the optimum timing—after three seconds the dog won't make the proper association that click means food).

3. Repeat until the treats are gone.

You shouldn't have to do this for more than two minutes. If your dog doesn't make the connection right away, don't think that you have a lemon—just do it longer. Some dogs may be nervous about strange new noises, so just in case your dog is one of those, put the clicker in your pocket to muffle the sound at first. If your dog runs away in fear the first time you click, don't use the clicker! Just use a "yes" as your click word. You'll just have to prime it longer than the clicker.

It All Starts With Eye Contact

In the same training session (after priming the clicker) you are now going to teach the dog to stare at you adoringly. Without eye contact, you can't teach the dog anything, so logistically, this is the next step in training. Most dogs will look at you after a few seconds — "Hello? Why did you stop feeding me?" And that's what you'll mark.

Again, have a handful of treats ready and the dog in front of you. Now follow these steps:

1. Wait for eye contact. Your dog may mug your hand, so, if needed, put your hands behind your back. Keep your eyes on your dog and just wait silently.

2. Be ready to click and treat. Usually after three to ten seconds, your dog will look up at your face.

3. The next time your dog looks at you, click and treat. On average, it takes dogs two to three minutes to figure out where the "magic button" is (looking at your face).

Repeat for a few minutes at a time, two-three times a day for two weeks and then a few times a week for the rest of the dog's life. If you have noticed, I haven't asked you to name this (eye contact). That is because it isn't necessary. Just train for it and

Making eye contact.
Photo: P. Dennison

your dog will be boring holes in your head automatically. If you name it, the dog will only look at you when you say your "look at me" cue. If your dog starts following you around all of the time, you're doing a great job!

My Name Is "No, No, Bad Dog!"—What's Yours?

Does your dog know his name? Or if he does, does he think that hearing his name is a bad thing? The fastest, easiest, most surefire way to teach your dog that his name is valuable and something to respond to instantly, is this (again, borrowing from Pavlov—name = reinforcement). In the same session that you've worked eye contact, you'll now add his name when he looks at your face.

     1. Have a few treats in your hand.

     2. When the dog gives you eye contact, say his name.

     3. Then click and treat.

Repeat for a few minutes at a time, two-three times a day for two weeks and then a few times a week for the rest of the dog's life.

The Art
If you always keep your hand in your pocket, then your dog won't look at you if your hand isn't in your pocket. Why? Because "hand in pocket" becomes a cue and it's not something we want to happen.

> ### Alert!
> You can very easily train your dog to ignore his name. Say that your dog is out in the yard and you want him in the house. You call his name. He ignores you. You continue to call his name repeatedly. Each time you yell it louder and louder and louder, hoping that if you scream his name at the top of your lungs, he will finally answer you. Guess what? He won't, and now he'll ignore his name whenever you use it. You can even do this with "Come" as well!

In the beginning stages, be sure you don't use the dog's name to get him to look at you—say his name after he looks at you. One way is nagging, the other is teaching. After a day or two, you should start to see the dog get whiplash looking at you when you say his name. If you just rescued your dog or you have truly poisoned your dog's name, this is the perfect time to change it.

After you've trained this for a few days, continue to keep eye contact strong. Every time you say the dog's name and he responds, reinforce him! "Good! You responded when I said your name! Brilliant doggie!" Be sure to heavily reinforce, especially when there are distractions around—then really go crazy and make him think that he won a million dollars worth of treats.

> ***Pointer***
> You can even make your smile into a reinforcer. I do this because I can't bring food into the obedience ring, so I use a smile as a reward. If the judges ever make us wear paper bags over our heads during competition, I'm in big trouble.

Praise Words

To drive up the value of your praise words (remember, these words are not naturally reinforcing for your dog), pair the words with food. You don't have to click for this one.

Say your praise word(s)—"Good dog," "Wahoo," "Yippee," "Excellent," and so on—and then treat within a half second. If you use many different ones (as I do), then say one word per session.

Because we talk to and around our dogs, and dogs are not a verbal species, speech tends to become white noise to them. You need to do this exercise for more than two minutes (as we did with the clicker). Continue to pair the praise word with food a few times per day for a few weeks.

The First Stage of "Come"

The most important thing you can teach your dog is to come reliably when called (also known as a recall). This behavior could save his life one day, so please don't skimp on your training of it. The first step to building a reliable "Come" is to continue to build your relationship, and be variable and unpredictable in how you reinforce his behavior.
I start training come as a stationary exercise.

The Science
I use a technique called "back-chaining," which teaches the last part of the behavior first. What's the last part of a recall? The dog will be in front of you.

1. Have a few treats in your hand and have the dog in front of you — sitting, standing, laying down — it doesn't matter.

2. When the dog gives you eye contact, say his name, then say "Come."

3. Click and treat.

4. Repeat for a few minutes per session, a few times per day for two weeks and then a few times per week for the rest of the dog's life.

In this session, I don't want you or the dog to actually move. You just want him to listen to the words while he's in front of you. If your dog has a history of ignoring the word "Come," feel free to change your word. "Here" is a popular recall word. For additional steps on teaching a recall, see Chapter 6.

Sit, Down, Stand

Sitting, lying down, and standing on cue are extremely useful behaviors. You can use them as alternate behaviors to jumping, for proper greeting behaviors, and for veterinarian visits, and they're the basis for many other behaviors. They're all easy to teach and there's very little your dog can do wrong when he's sitting or lying down. The key to teaching the basic behaviors in this section is to associate the correct

> ### *Alert!*
> When teaching any behavior, it's vital that you don't say the word before the behavior happens. It's imperative that you add the word for the behavior at precisely the correct time — as the dog is doing it. If you say the word "Sit" while the dog is standing, then what behavior have you named "Sit"? The stand! For those of you that may want to know more about this — it's called Backward conditioning and will never produce what you're looking for. See the appendix for "Learning and Behavior" by Paul Chance.

word with the behavior you want. Your dog is running around the yard and you call him to "Come." He doesn't know the meaning of the word, and yet you keep calling him anyway. He is running around, playing with a toy, urinating, barking and digging, while you scream "Come!" The next time you say "Come," he will say to you, "I know what that means!" and run around, play with a toy, urinate, bark, and dig. Why? Because those were the behaviors you paired with the word "Come."

"Sit"

1. Put a treat in your hand and hold your hand up over the dog's head (canine physics in action here—head goes up, butt goes down!). I recommend having your palm facing up for this signal.

2. Do not say "Sit" before the dog sits.

3. When his hind end hits the floor, say "Sit."

4. Then click and treat.

5. If the dog jumps up, simply take your hand away and try again, perhaps lowering your signal hand.

6. Repeat a few times with a treat in your hand.

7. Then take the treat out of your hand and continue to give your new hand signal (palm up).

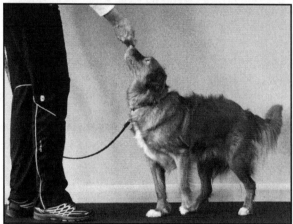

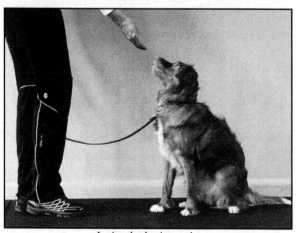

Luring the dog into a sit.

Photos: T. Hirsch

8. For now, until the dog learns the behavior, continue to say the word "Sit" as the dog's hind end hits the ground.

Alert!

When you start to say the word before the behavior, be sure to say it only once. Don't get sucked into the trap of saying "Sit" repeatedly in the hope that the dog might finally understand. Saying the cue word repeatedly will only teach the dog to respond after the fifth "Sit." Remember; sit is one syllable and sitsitsitsitsit is five syllables.

Say your signal word and then wait for at least 10 seconds. You can say it one more time and wait again for 10 full seconds. If the dog still doesn't respond, go back to using the hand signal a few more times.

It's important to get the food out of your signal hand as soon as possible, because otherwise the dog is just following the treat. I don't mind using a lure (dog is following your hand with the treat in it) as long as that hand motion then becomes the cue. Usually you can start saying the word before the behavior after about a week or two of practicing a few sessions per day. And by that time you can just randomly reinforce the sit — you won't need to treat for each and every one.

Down

You can teach the "Down" in the same noninvasive way. Please don't push down on your dog's shoulders or yank him down by the collar. This would only stress him out, or at the very least, make him more resistant to lying down because you're activating his opposition reflex. Here's what to do instead:

1. Have a treat in your hand.

2. Ask the dog to "Sit."

3. Bring your hand (slowly) straight down to the ground.

4. When the dog lies down (not before), say "Down"; then click and treat.

5. Repeat a few times until the dog is lying down faster, and then take the food out of your signal hand, as you did with the "Sit."

Definition

Opposition reflex is the natural reflexive action that makes a dog push or pull against anything that is pushing or pulling against him.

If your dog doesn't lie down right away, make the steps smaller and use tiny approximations. Try this at first on a slippery floor rather than on carpeting.

1. When your dog lowers his head to follow your hand, treat (no click yet — withhold the click until you get the finished behavior).

2. When he lowers his head more, treat.

3. After a few repetitions, start to watch his shoulders. Hold your hand steady on the floor. As his shoulders start to lower, treat.

4. Continue in this vein and then treat when both shoulders are lowered.

5. Usually by this point, on the next try, your dog will lie down. Be sure to click and jackpot with lots of treats.

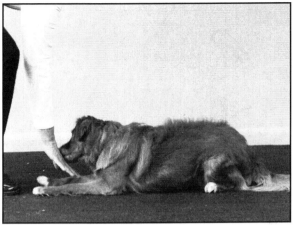

Luring the dog into a down.
Photos: T. Hirsch

You should see the light bulb come on in your dog's eyes after a few more repetitions and he'll start to lie down faster and faster.

If your dog won't lie down using this method, don't think that you have a stupid dog; he just doesn't understand what you want. You can try this:

1. Sit on the ground with your leg up, forming a "tent" with your knee. (If your dog is too big to fit under your knee, you can use a chair or table instead.)

2. Have some treats in both hands.

3. Lure the dog under your knee.

4. Do not push the dog down with your leg.

5. Once the dog's shoulder is under your leg, slowly raise your hand with the treat so that his head follows. Usually he'll lie down at this point.

6. Be sure to say "Down" and then click and treat.

Repeat a bunch of times until the dog lies down fairly quickly. Now you'll have to fade out your knee:

1. Sit on the floor and don't raise your knee.

2. Move your hand in the same motion, as if you're luring your dog under your leg, but lure next to your leg.

3. When your dog lies down, say "Down," and click and treat.

Once the dog is lying down with a minimum lure from you, you can go back to the earlier steps and lure from a "Sit."

I'm sure you've been bending over or kneeling on the ground, so now is the time to start changing your cue to just a hand signal. Otherwise, you'll have to bend over for the rest of the dog's life. Here's what to do:

1. Ask your dog to "Sit."

2. Stand up straight and bring your signal hand down to the ground. Hold it there until the dog lies down. Then click and treat.

3. Repeat, but this time, bring your hand down to only about two inches off the ground and hold it there. Your dog will probably look at you in confusion, but hold your position. He may also mug your hand. Just stay still. He will lie down. Click and treat when he does.

4. The next step is to bend over so that your hand is now about four inches from the ground. Wait again until your dog lies down. Click and treat when he does.

5. Continue in this vein until you're standing straight and just doing a simple hand motion without bending over. Be sure to stand up straighter only about two inches at a time.

Do these steps over a few days. Don't forget: too much drilling can be seen as a form of punishment by the dog. If for some reason your dog still isn't understanding what you want, you can simply wait until he does it on his own and then click and treat.

The Art & Science

This (the waiting for the dog to do a natural behavior on his own) is called "cap-turing." As with the "Sit," be sure to continue to say the word "Down" as the dog is lying down, not before. It usually takes about two weeks for the dog to learn the behavior reliably. At that time you can then start to say the word "Down" before the behavior and as with the sit, go to a random reinforcement schedule once the dog truly understands it.

When practicing "Sit" and "Down," try not to always do them in the same order. Dogs notice patterns. You may think the dog knows the behavior, but he doesn't—he only knows the order in which the behaviors are performed. If you always ask for a "Sit" and then a "Down," and now you ask for a "Down" from a "Stand," your dog may look at you blankly. You don't have a stupid dog, you just pattern trained him. So mix it up and keep him guessing and interested.

A handler standing straight up, using a hand signal to tell the dog to go "Down."

Photo: P. Dennison

Alert!

You may start to notice that your dog responds better to your hand signal than to your verbal signal. Dogs are more attuned to their physical environment, which includes our body language. Learning what our spoken words mean is harder for them to figure out than what our hand signals mean.

"Stand"

"Stand" is useful for grooming, nail clipping, and vet visits. And if you want to compete with your dog at shows, "Stand" is a must. Here's how to teach him:

1. Have your dog in a "Sit" position on your left side.

2. Put your right hand in front of the dog's nose and slowly lure him, with a treat in your flat hand, parallel to the ground, into the standing position.

3. Be sure not to say "Stand" until he does the behavior. As soon as he stands, say "Stand," and then click and treat.

After a few repetitions, get the treat out of your hand. Be sure to continue to keep your hand flat. Don't forget: dogs watch our body language, and a curled hand looks different from a flat hand.

After a few days, you should be able to give the hand signal and say the word "Stand" before the behavior. As with the "Sit" and "Down," don't repeat it a second time. You can just hold your position and wait for the dog to think. If after 10 full seconds he doesn't "Stand," then just start over with the earlier steps for a day or two.

Holding the treat properly when luring into the "Stand."....The dog is now standing.
Photos: T. HirscH

You can start to add petting into the "Stand" in preparation for handling and grooming. Begin with a gentle touch, and gradually add real petting.

Pop Quiz

1. What is opposition reflex?

2. How many "Sits" or "Downs" (or other good behaviors) does your dog do before you reward him?

3. Why is it a good idea not to ask for the same behaviors in exactly the same order?

4. Why is the word "no" useless? What should you say instead?

5. Have you trained your dog (in the past) to ignore his name or your "come" cue? If so, what is your new "come" word?

6. Why is it a good idea not to name the behavior of eye contact?

7. What is the definition of a learned behavior?

Summary

The foundation of good training is first building a positive relationship with your dog.

Start training by priming the clicker, teaching eye contact, name response and come.

Teaching your dog to come when called is important in later training and could one day save his or her life.

Have fun with your dog—continue to add to the piggy bank of your relationship.

Hands-off training will get you there faster.

Verbal and Whistle Recall   6

Many people have come to me, telling me they "just want to teach my dog to come when called." While that's a great and of course understandable goal, there is no such thing as "just" when teaching a recall. Coming when called is not a single behavior, like a sit. Reliably coming when called is based on many different variables and has its roots in;

- Your relationship with your dog,

- Your reinforcement history,

- How often you practice with and without distractions.

- How well you can read his body language, to tell if this instant is the right time to call him to you,

- How often you call your dog when he has no intention of coming (which, in essence, allows him to practice not coming).

Whether you know it or not, you've already started working on the recall with the exercise eye contact-name-come from the stationary position outlined in Chapter 5. Now we'll add in the movement. I will be showing you how to teach a verbal recall, as well as a whistle recall. If you are a more visual person, my Maxwell award winning Training the Whistle Recall DVD is in the appendix.

Recall: The "basic recipe"
For this behavior alone, do not phase out the food or other reinforcers—ever, for the life of the dog. Reinforcers can be petting, praise, food, a rousing game of tug. Whatever the dog loves, do them all!

Make your "Come" signal distinct (not sometimes "C'mere," sometimes "Come," sometimes "Here," sometimes "Let's Go," and so on). In the beginning stages of the recall, don't say the word unless your dog is already on his way to you! You must pair the word with the specific behavior of the dog racing to you for the dog to learn exactly what "Come" means.

Say "Come" only when you're prepared to reinforce heavily—for at least 20 seconds! If you don't have anything on you, you can run to the reinforcers, all the

eping his attention on you, whooping and praising.
Make sure the dog comes within a few inches—do not reach out to feed the dog, otherwise you risk teaching your dog to actually stay away from you.

Benefits of whistle training

The whistle recall is a great tool for many reasons:

- The whistle can be heard over nature's sounds — surf, thunder, rain, and even man-made sounds, like a generator, loud trucks, etc.

- The whistle is never annoyed, never angry, never scared or panicked; It sounds the same every time

- If you have have ruined your "Come" cue with previous ineffective or incorrect training, the whistle is a great alternative (or in addition to a verbal recall)

- If the dog gets lost or is out of sight, the whistle sound travels much farther than a verbal recall

- If your dog is starting to lose his hearing, the whistle will often be heard.

Priming the whistle

Just like you primed the clicker, you'll need to prime the whistle. Each and every day for 14 days, you will "prime" the whistle. Blow the whistle in this pattern — two short blasts and one really long blast and then treat your dog (no clicker). Two-three minutes per session, rapid fire whistle/treat, three times per day.

This step is extremely important because we are looking to create a conditioned response: Whistle = Rewards. No "cheating!" You may be tempted to condition the whistle for a few days and try to actually use it as a recall signal before the dog is trained to respond. Please don't — there is no shortcut to learning this properly.

The "Drop-the-Cookie-and-Run-Like-Heck" Game

This is a wonderful "Come" game that both you and your dog will love. And you get to continue to build that positive relationship because all these training exercises are fun!
Follow these steps:

1. Throw a cookie a few feet away. (Make sure the dog sees it!)
2. Tell your dog to "Get it." (very important to give him permission to get it)
3. Run away from him fast!

As the dog is coming to you, stop running, turn and face him, while saying "Come" or whistle (pairing the word or sound with the behavior). Don't use a verbal and a whistle at the same time. Rotate between the verbal or the whistle.

Dropping the cookie ...and running like heck (and calling your dog to "Come" as he is coming)...

Photos: T. Hirsch

...and reinforce at the end.
Photos: T. Hirsch

Alert!
When you are calling your dog, use a happy
voice. Don't be your mother ("Richard!
You are really in for it now! I said, come
here, now!!!" Stamp, stamp!), be Ed
McMahon ("Zelda! You just won a million
dollars in Publisher's Clearing House!!!!!
Wahoo! Come and get your check!")

When he gets to you, click and treat
with a jackpot. Jackpots are given for
every recall and are fed one cookie
at a time. To a dog, a wad of treats is
the same as one treat, so spread them
out and keep him with you longer. Be
variable in the number of treats. Add in
play, petting and praise as well.

Definition
A jackpot is lots of treats given to the dog, one at a time. I like to give a jackpot when
the dog has done something hard for the very first time, or if a behavior is particularly
wonderful. For some reason, many people think three is a magic number of treats as a
jackpot. Think slot machine - would you consider three quarters to be a jackpot?

Build up your reinforcement history and your dog will remember just how generous
you are, especially when it really matters. Two or three treats is not a jackpot. When I
heavily reinforce my own dogs, I use 10-30 treats.

"Drop the cookie and don't run" game

This game should also be practiced without running. Just throw the treat farther
away and wait for the dog to get it. Once he finds the treat, whistle or verbally
call the dog back. If you always run away, the dog will think that the recall signal
entails someone running away. This step will get your dog out of that possible
misconception. Be sure to use big chunks of white cheese or chicken when working
outside — otherwise the dog won't find the treat in the grass.

For those of you with families, I recommend playing a nice game of "Round Robin."
Everyone has a whistle, and one at a time, each family member whistles the dog
to them (or says dog's name and then whistles as he's coming to you, not before),
heavily reinforces and then the next person whistles. The dogs love it, the kids love

it, and the dog learns to respond appropriately to the entire family. An additional perk is a really tired dog and everyone knows that a tired dog is a good dog!

The "Let your dog get distracted" game

After about two weeks of these exercises, we begin to phase out the tossing of the treat. Otherwise your dog may think throwing a treat and/or running away is part of the cue and won't come unless you've thrown a treat or run away.

The Art

You play only the "Toss the cookie and run" game and then don't train the additional steps. You're not thinking ahead to what cue the dog is actually picking up on. I had a student not take it further and to this day, the dog won't come unless she's running away — not very convenient when it's inclement weather.

So whatever behavior you're teaching, look at your body language and assume that to the dog, it will become part of the cue. For instance, if you typically kneel down when calling your dog and then don't, don't be surprised when he doesn't come — because to him, the picture is now different.

The next step is to be boring (off leash in a safe place) for a few minutes and let your dog get distracted. Say only his name, with the tone of a question mark in it. If he responds by looking back at you, call or whistle him in and jackpot. Practice this in a relatively benign area — few distractions to start.

The "Liar's Game"

"Come with distractions" is probably the most important behavior you will teach the dog. There are many different games we can use to teach this essential response. This game teaches the dog that YOU are always a "sure bet" and everyone else in the world is a liar.

Part One:

- Toss the treat far. Your "liar" will stand in between you and your dog with a treat or a low value toy. The liar has something of relatively low value to the dog because we want to set him up for success!

- You run across the room or yard

- Call (verbally to start) dog to come

- The liar tries to distract the dog. The liar does NOT let the dog have any goodies or give eye contact

- Do NOT repeat your cue – just wait

- When dog looks at you, whistle him in or call him verbally and treat with a huge jackpot

- Repeat until the dog is actively avoiding the liar.

Dog running toward me...passing the liar...coming to me!

Photos: E. Jaborska

Part two:
Increase the amount of the distractions – for instance, add a dog to the environment, making sure that your dog cannot get to the other dog or another such high value reinforcer. When your dog comes, click and give a huge jackpot. Then as an additional bonus prize, you can let the recalled dog play with the other one!

Increase the value of the objects that the Liar has, making sure that YOUR jackpots raise in value also. Add some additional Liars and have a few people trying to distract the dog away from his mission of coming to you.

Warning on the Liars Game: Do not use family members as Liars!

> ***Alert!***
> Be sure to use your "come" cue only for a recall. Don't dilute it by using it for loose-leash walking or anything else.

Play Hide-and-Seek
Have someone hold your dog while you run away and hide. Then call the dog. The instant you say the dog's name ("Fluffy"...), your helper should drop the leash. When you hear him on his way, then you can add in your recall word (or whistle). When the dog finds you, have a huge party with all sorts of reinforcers.

Just as you won't call your dog in the beginning stages of training the recall unless he's on his way, don't whistle unless you know for a fact that your dog is coming. Otherwise your dog will learn to ignore the whistle.

Or if you're alone, just run and hide while the dog is in another room, and then call him. I do this with my dogs—it's pretty funny with three dogs in a teeny tiny house, all skidding around trying to get to me first.

Walking in a Field or Trail
Bring your fanny pack, some toys and treats, and a long leash — preferably a 15 to 20 foot line. Before the dog gets to the end of the line, say his name—once. You don't want his name associated with a painful pop on the collar, which is why you do it before he hits the end of the leash. Better still if you put a harness on him to avoid any tracheal, spinal or neck damage.

The Art
Once you've been practicing for a few weeks, call or whistle before he checks in. And here's where knowing his body language will help. There is a real knack (art) for recognizing when is a good time and when is a bad time to try this. Be attentive to

potentially high distractions, so as not to attempt the recall when the dog might be in conflict. Set up for success!

The Science
When NOT to call dog: Did you know that when a dog is sniffing and their mouths are closed, their ears are also essentially closed; in other words, they literally can't hear you. Weird, but true. Why am I telling you this? Because if a dog is sniffing, don't call/whistle until his mouth is open and his head is up.

Call/Whistle the dog in when he isn't sniffing (at first), heavily reward and release the dog to go back to whatever he wants to do (which is also a reward). Go on with your walk, periodically whistling him in.

Tip: Go to the home page on my website, www.pamdennison.com scroll down to the bottom and watch the "Black and White Club" video clips. You'll see it in action — where we all whistle and our dogs all come to their owners.

What if my dog doesn't respond?
At this point, if you've been diligently practicing, he should. However, if he doesn't, don't repeat the verbal/whistle — just wait and judge a better time to whistle him in. If you try a second time and your dog still ignores it, just go back a few steps. He's telling you he hasn't built up a conditioned response to the cue yet.

If he responds by turning his head to you, say "Come," or whistle. When he comes to you, click once and treat heavily. Continue to practice this as you continue your walk. If he doesn't respond to his name, then don't say it again right now. Wait until you really think he will respond—this would not be when his entire head is down in a gopher hole.

> ### Details
> You don't want the dog to get used to taking one cookie and then running away from you because he knows you pay out only one cookie. One day he'll be distracted by something more interesting than your one cookie, such as a squirrel. Chasing that squirrel could lead him into the path of a truck. Pay heavily now for reliability later!

Adding Distractions
Get yourself a 20 to 50-foot-long line and practice, in tons of locations where there are distractions, all of the "Come" behaviors listed above. You can't exercise a dog properly on a six-foot leash, so the long line becomes a portable fence!

The heavier the distractions, the larger and more exciting your reinforcers should be. Start with small distractions that are far away, and gradually build to greater ones that are closer.

You can practice this method with many distractions—not all at one time, of course. You don't want to allow your dog to chase cars, but you can still train an instant recall for when he's aroused by using "safe" and highly valued distractions. If your dog loves to chase cars, he may also love to chase balls or Frisbees. You can use his high arousal to toys (instead of speeding cars) to train for instant recall. Teach your dog to come off a toy in the midst of chasing it by following these steps:

1. Have the dog off leash in a safe area or on a 20 to 50-foot-long line with it dragging. Start off with the very lowest valued item you can think of, such as a paper-towel tube.

2. Throw the tube.

3. Tell the dog to "Get It."

4. As the dog goes toward it—just a step or two—call or whistle him back to you and heavily reward him with toys he likes, petting, praise, or food.

5. Throw the tube again and repeat a few times until he's running back to you at top speed.

6. Now find another item, slightly more valued than the tube. Repeat the exercise, always rewarding heavily for the recall. Gradually increase the value of the thrown toy while increasing the value of your rewards when he comes back to you.

7. If at any point your dog ignores you and ends up getting the toy, don't say anything—just stand there passively, count to five, and start over. Don't block the dog or become a barrier.

A Border Collie coming away from a tennis ball.

Photo by P. Dennison

This is not about "obedience" (How dare he not come back to me?); this is about building your relationship, so that your dog wants to play this game with you, and wants to come off a toy, bike, car, deer, because playing with you is fun to do.

Continue in short sessions—three to five throws of the object per session—until you're using the highest-valued toy imaginable and your dog is making skid marks in the grass to come back to you. Periodically, allow him to get to the toy without calling him back to you, play with him with the toy, and then work your recall again. The more practice you can do with your recalls with safe objects when the dog is aroused, the more easily he will come off inappropriate objects when in that same state.

Pop Quiz

1. In the beginning stages, why is it a good idea not to call or whistle to your dog unless he is already on his way to you?

2. If your dog comes away from something really interesting (like a squirrel or deer), even if it is 10 minutes later, what should you do?

Summary

Prime the whistle each and every day, two-three times per day for 14 solid days before playing the "come" games. In the beginning stages, be sure to call or whistle only when your dog is on his way to you.

Vary your reinforcement types — food, toys, play — all are rewarding!

Animal Husbandry 7

It isn't a Veterinarian's or Groomer's job to teach their animal patients how to accept different types of handling, and many untrained dogs can become aggressive during a visit. Their job is to get their job done as quickly as possible. Your job is to teach your dog to accept the handling needed.

You may have a dog that needs to be muzzled and handled firmly (and not so nicely) for their annual visit. Some become so aggressive that you can't handle them at all unless they are tranquilized. Trying to work with a dog like this can be dangerous — not just to you, but to the dog as well, because if you can't handle them, then you can't give them medical care either.

Petting and Handling

Repetition of calm behaviors is one of the building blocks to a healthy and happy relationship with your dog.

It's important to remember that uninvited hands or faces reaching down toward a dog's head can be seen, from the dog's perspective, as being aggressive. As a consequence, a large percentage of dog bites happen to children because children enthusiastically push themselves abruptly into a dog's face. You don't have to just "put up with" your dog's dislike of handling—you can train him to accept it, but at the same time understand that you must, at times, protect him as well.

You think that your dog needs to be bathed and brushed, and he thinks otherwise. He bites you or the brush, or he may not even let you get that far—he may run away at the sight of anything that even looks like a grooming implement. And toenail clipping? Forget about it!

Details

Louise came in with her dog Teddy, with her arms bloody and scratched. Teddy didn't like petting at all and would tell her so in a not-nice way. After one week of working with Teddy, he allowed Louise to pet him. We taught him to enjoy petting by pairing a light touch with treats. After the second week, Teddy was actively enjoying having Louise pet him. (See more about the Premack principle in Chapter 13.)

The first step to teaching your dog how to handle unwanted attention with a minimum of stress is to begin slowly and carefully. An additional side benefit is that as you "work" with your dog in this way, you build trust and establish a kind of communication that makes your training with him easier as you move into more advanced tasks. Before starting these sessions, you must first practice the behaviors as instructed in Chapter 5; priming the clicker, eye contact, "Sit," "Down," "Stand."

chin   nose twch to hand

The goal of the following exercises is to reinforce no movement and acceptance from the dog while you touch and hold him. Start your session by giving your dog a few treats to get his attention. Break the training session into two or three sessions of approximately five minutes each. If your dog seems to be getting antsy, shorten the session to 2 minutes. Keep your sessions short and successful—just a few minutes at a time. Be sure to include all family members in the touching sessions—not all at once, but one at a time.

The Art

The key here is to stop before the dog gets nervous or is about to nip or bite you. If that happens, you've gone too far and some trust is lost. Break handling down into it's smallest of components if you need to. When I've worked with dogs that have serious handling issues, I've had to approximate the steps into minuscule pieces. If a light touch with one finger is too much for the dog, then perhaps he can deal with a "fake" touch with one finger, where you're not actually touching the dog. The art is to be able to read the dog, to "feel" the dog, so you can teach him and be safe at the same time.

One arm around dog

Both arms around dog

One arm around dog, palm of hand on dog's cheek

One arm around dog, hand flat under chin, holding it up for jugular blood draw

One hand under dog's chin for jugular blood draw, one finger tapping

Both arms over dog, moving head away gently

One hand under chin, one hand on top of dog's muzzle

One hand under chin, one hand gently lifting top lip to show teeth

Photo Series: T. Hirsch

Now follow these "basic recipe" steps: (don't use the clicker for these—too cumbersome unless you have a second person to help you)

1. With your dog sitting or standing, place one arm around the dog. If he doesn't move, say "yes" and give him a treat. Repeat about five to six times.

2. Place both arms around dog. As long as he doesn't struggle, say "yes" and give him a treat. Repeat five to six times.

3. Place one arm around dog and with the palm of your hand, put that hand on his cheek (not his muzzle) and bring his face in toward your armpit. Say "yes" and treat. Repeat five to six times.

4. With the dog standing, place both arms over the dog, using your upper arm to bring his head behind you (so his teeth are away from anyone's face). Say "yes" if he doesn't move and give him a treat. Repeat five to six times.

5. Place one arm around dog's chest and put the palm of your other hand under his chin and lift up, move his face to the right and left, say "yes" if he doesn't move, treat and release. You will want to practice this one just in case you ever need to get a blood draw from his jugular vein.

6. Once he is comfortable with step five, add in tapping his jugular vein (or thereabouts) to get him used to it.

Make sure you practice all of these steps for at least two weeks and have friends help you. It is all good that you can handle your dog, but you need to make sure that strangers (vets, technicians and groomers) can handle your dog as well.

There may be times when you will need to grab your dog's collar-leashes break, someone lets the dog out by mistake, or the dog ends up in a dangerous situation where all bets are off. Teach your dog to accept these next steps and it may just save his life one day. These are not about scruff shakes and alpha rolls — they are about keeping your dog safe and comfortable with all types of handling.

"Collar" (noun)

I start out teaching the dog that "collar" is a noun. Later on, we'll make it a verb. To do this, touch the collar, say "collar"/treat/release. Repeat five to six times. Be sure to grab from many different directions — underneath, side and on top. That way, if a stranger tries to grab your dog before he runs out into the street, your dog will think, "oh goodie, cookie time!"

Those of you with little dogs will really appreciate this exercise — no more chasing the little ones around!

"Collar" (verb)

After repeating the above step — touch collar, say "collar" and treat at least 30 times, hold your hand out a few inches away from the collar and say "collar" and see what your dog does. He should move his neck into your hand. Repeat this a few times and build some distance — a few inches at a time. The goal here is that if you say "collar" your dog will move to place his neck in your hand, thus making "collar" a verb!

Leash and "collar"

Raise your hand if, when you take your dog off leash, or the collar slips off, your dog takes that as a cue to run away?

> **Details**
> I practice this with my own dogs while walking on the trail. Instead of calling all three dogs by name, I just stretch my hand out and say "collar" and all of them come running.

1. Put the leash on your dog while saying "collar." Give the dog a treat (no clicking needed)

2. Take the leash off as you're saying "collar" and give the dog a treat.

Repeat those two steps dozens of times and you'll see that once you take the leash off, your dog won't leave you unless you verbally release them to do so.

"Collar" (lead)

Now take hold of the collar, saying "collar" and gently lead your dog a few feet, using a treat as a lure to start. As long as he doesn't struggle, say "yes" and treat/release. This comes in handy when you catch the dog but forgot in your panic to grab the leash. Be sure not to drag your dog by the collar — he will resist!

Scruff (lead)

The collar may slip off one day and all of a sudden you have a naked loose dog. So practice gently grabbing his scruff/hair, "yes" and treat. Once he is comfortable with this, as in the step above, start to lead him while holding onto his scruff.

> **Pointer**
> Let's say you have a big dog or one that you can't pick up or that your dog got loose and you were able to catch him, but in your terror, forgot a leash. And let's say that you're too far from home or car to lead him by the collar or scruff. Without knowing it, you may already have a solution! If you're wearing a belt, use your belt as a leash. Every woman I know, knows how to take their bra off without taking their shirt off, so you can use your bra as a leash! Who cares if it looks funny?

Belly

There are also times when you will need to check out his belly and pubic areas for fleas, ticks and rash patrol.

Very gently, roll your puppy over and rub his belly, say "yes" if he doesn't resist and give him a treat. If he does resist, let him nibble the treat as you lure him over while gently pushing. This is not about being dominant to/over him! He should become accustomed to this pretty quickly and allow you to roll him over without incident.

If your dog won't let you gently nudge him over, don't get into a tizzy — just train him to "settle." (see later in this chapter). I rescue all of my dogs and in the beginning, not one of them would let me nudge them, so I trained the "settle" as outlined.

Brushing and touching

Some dogs don't like to be brushed, and must be taught to like it. For the very young pup, you can slather something gooey (like peanut butter or cream cheese) on the refrigerator and let him lick it while you gently brush or pet with a light stroke. Stop before he's done licking. You can do this in the bathtub as well. Get him used to all different kinds of touching and handling as early as possible.

In addition to the above exercises, place your hand gently along the side of the dog's face. Once he's comfortable with that, you can add in head touching and then slowly add in each body part: ears, tail, face, back of his neck and shoulders, each leg, foot, toes, gums and teeth. If you have a breed of dog that will need regular grooming (not just a bath), you will have to do some extra conditioning. For instance, if your dog has a beard, be sure to teach him to accept the holding of his beard. If your dog has hair that will grow over his eyes, you'll need to teach him to accept scissors coming toward his eyes. For this one, use your finger first, then a pencil, and then scissors. Groomers are people, too, and don't have magic wands to miraculously make your dog into a pleasure to groom. Practice these maneuvers and your groomer will thank you!

Repeat these exercises a few times per day for a few weeks, touching all body parts gently. Once he likes gentle petting, you can gradually add rougher petting. You can even teach the dog to accept pinching (which is a similar sensation to getting an injection), by using this method.

One foot, two foot, green foot, blue foot

I love this exercise for two reasons;

1. It gets the dog used to their feet being picked up, which will in turn help with toe nail clipping and any other kind of foot exam.

2. It's actually a core building exercise for the dogs. We often forget that our dogs need to build strength in certain areas of their bodies to avoid injury. My human chiropractor said his business is very busy after the first snowfall, because people don't typically exercise year-round to keep their core strong.

When picking up feet, especially a back one, remember that dogs don't naturally know how to stand on three legs. Place your other hand gently under his belly to give him some support. Once the dog gets the hang of it, you won't need to help him keep from falling over.

The Art

Be careful and go slowly. If you let go, you are reinforcing the struggling. If you don't let go, you may freak him out. The best course is to go slowly enough so that the dog likes being handled. Redirect with a treat if needed. The key here is to slowly build up to complete body touching so that the dog wouldn't even think about moving away. I actually don't use food for this one, unless your dog already has a bad association to feet touching. If you need to, have a second person feed while you pick up each foot.

1. Gently pick up a back leg and when you feel your dog balance himself, gently put it down

2. Do the same thing with each leg, making sure you keep the leg underneath him — don't bring the leg out to the side.

3. Once your dog is comfortable with this, pick up the right back leg, wait for him to balance and then gently pick up the left front leg. He'll be balancing on two legs.

4. Then do the opposite — left rear leg and right front leg.

Lifting one foot at a time, while supporting the dog.

Photos: T. Hirsch

Lifting the right front leg and left rear leg. Then left front leg and right rear leg. Notice how the legs are underneath the dog, not out to the side.

Photos: T. Hirsch

This may take quite a few sessions depending on how sensitive your dog is to handling. Don't rush, and don't get angry—these emotions will always get you in trouble.

Toe nails

If you know how to clip nails without cutting the "quick" (blood supply), that's great. Work on all of the handling exercises above and you should be just fine. If however, you're nervous, squeamish, or not sure exactly where the quick is, don't even try to clip your dog's nails. You can see the quick more easily on a dog with white nails. If your dog has black nails, you'll be working blind.

If you decide that you want to clip your dog's nails yourself, just cut off the tip of them at first. If you're nervous at all—just one iota of nervousness—do not, I repeat, do not clip your dog's nails. All it takes is one "Oh my god, I made you bleed!" while you run around screaming hysterically, to turn your dog into a toenail demon. You can still teach the dog to accept this and leave the actual clipping to a professional.

Luring the dog into a "Settle."
Photos: T. Hirsch

"Settle" and "Roll Over"

"Settle" means to have the dog lie down on his side and stay there. You may also call it "Rest," or "Flat." "Roll over" is obvious—the dog rolls over. Both of these behaviors are useful in handling, grooming, and vet visits.

flat

"Settle" is a great behavior for the dog to learn. The uses are many: veterinarian visits, calming behaviors, tick and flea patrol, checking rashes, taking out burrs or any type of physical exam you may need to do. Here's how to teach your dog:

1. Have the dog in a "Down."

2. Place your hand with a treat in front of the dog's nose.

3. Lure his head around slowly so that his nose is now facing his rear end.

4. When his elbow buckles underneath him, move the treat slowly around so that his head is flat on the ground. Click and treat.

5. If the dog gets up, don't worry; just try again.

Right now your hand cue is a big circle, but you can quickly change it to just be a small circle with your hand or finger. To get the "Stay" part of this exercise, use your pointer finger touching the ground as a helper cue, and then feed the treats from that hand. Fade out the treats in that hand as quickly as possible. It usually takes only a few days.

Once the dog is comfortable with the "Settle," you can add gentle petting or an exam of genital areas and feet, always clicking and treating the dog for not moving. If the dog moves away, just try again—perhaps you went too fast or were petting in a place that he's uncomfortable with.

You can also be very creative when adding a cue word for this and other trick behaviors. Think about it ahead of time so that you can add the cue word or hand motion from the beginning. My absolute favorite line is, "I am going to hypnotize you. When I count to three and snap my fingers, you will fall asleep. One, two, three (snap)." The snapping of your fingers is the cue for the dog to "Settle."

"Roll over" is the obvious next step after teaching the "Settle." "Roll over" is a great behavior to teach because it gets the dog acclimated to someone leaning over him. Here's what to do:

1. Once your dog is in the "Down" position, use the same luring movement that you started with doing the "Settle."

2. Now, instead of luring your dog's head to lie flat on the ground, continue to lure so that he rolls over completely. This may mean (depending on the size of dog you have) that you'll have to lean over him.

3. As soon as he rolls over, click and treat.

If he doesn't roll over right away or is nervous about your leaning over him, be sure to break down the steps into smaller ones. At each step of his head moving in the correct direction, treat. Be sure to move your hand slowly, and try not to get too excited about him "getting it" instantly. Small steps in easy training sessions will keep him interested in the game.

Summary
Work on the different holds for vet and groomer visits.

If you have a dog with facial hair, be sure to desensitize them to scissors and beard holding.

Make sure you teach him to accept holding each foot up in preparation to toenail clipping

Loose - Leash Walking   ꝏ

Because loose-leash walking is such an important topic and one that most people are desperate for, I've devoted this entire chapter to it. I've known some fantastic dogs who have been dumped in shelters just because they pull on the leash. There are many nuances to walking on a loose leash; as with come, loose leash walking is not a simple behavior, nor is it a single behavior. You can't *just* teach your dog to walk on a loose leash — there are many other facets to training this exercise and things that need to be trained before you can get the dog to walk on a loose leash.

Why Dogs Pull

You want to peacefully walk your dog, but your dog suddenly picks up a scent and takes off at warp speed. Your walks have become such a nightmare that you almost wish you could undo his housetraining because cleaning up messes on the carpet would be easier than walking him.

A dog taking his owner for a walk.
Photo: P. Dennison

You sweat, you yank back, in desperation you use a choke or prong collar, you curse and scream. Finally, you declare your dog stupid, stubborn, willful, disobedient, or even "dominant." What has actually happened is that you've systematically trained your dog to pull on the leash. Congratulations! You did it! You learned how to activate his opposition reflex and taught him that to get where he wants to go, all he has to do is to pull you down the street.

Dogs do not pull to drive you insane, nor do they pull "because they can," and they truly haven't been up all night, scheming in their doggie minds how to annoy you to death by giving you whiplash. Really.

However, there are very specific reasons why dogs pull on the leash and do a great imitation of dislocating your shoulder.

Because We Follow

The number-one reason why dogs pull on the leash is this: because we follow. Behavior is reward-driven. If choking himself gets him what he wants—to move forward in any direction he so chooses—then guess what? He'll continue to pull.

Pulling on the leash then becomes a learned behavior, and a very strong one at that. "Fanatical" and "overzealous" are words that can be used to describe many dogs' leash—wrenching techniques, as they perfect their performance.

To Get to the Other Side

The number-two reason why dogs pull on the leash is to get to the other side. There are actually two parts to this. Part A: the outside world is an exciting and wonderfully smelly place for a dog. It is a veritable smorgasbord of scent. And Part B: the dog forgets that we exist and we are no more important than a speck of dust. There are many reasons for this seeming lack of respect. Most people train their dogs in the living room and never "take it on the road." They're then shocked and dismayed that their dog "blows them off" once outside. But it's not really personal — it's just another training issue.

> ### Details
> Did you know that a dog has 20 to 40 times more olfactory receptors than a human? Specially trained scent detecting dogs can find bodies, dead or alive, by following scents of shed skin flakes, sweat droplets, and scent mists for as a long as 105 hours and as far as 135 miles. Some service dogs can also "fore-smell" seizures in humans, alert a diabetic to high or low blood sugar level, and some have been trained to detect cancer cells.

Scent is extremely important to a dog—after all, they're predators. Yes, even a Maltese or Miniature Poodle. Dogs process a great deal of information about their world through their noses. We've all seen our dogs sniff one single blade of grass for 15 minutes and we think that this is a bit excessive. However, it's not without meaning for a dog. He finds out who was here and when, male or female, how old, their state of health, sexually intact or altered and most likely what the dog had for breakfast. For the dog, this is enormously interesting information.

The Art
That challenge can be drudgery or with the right attitude, it can be fun, enlightening, and immensely rewarding. The key here is the fundamental tenet of positive dog

training: the relationship between you and your dog. There are many subtleties and ways to build a bond with your dog.

Opposition Reflex

The number-three reason why dogs pull on the leash is this: because we activate their opposition reflex, which causes them to pull against anything that's pulling against them. Try this test: Have someone stand next to you. Push on their arm. If they don't want to fall, they will push back. Now pull on their arm. If they don't want to be yanked toward you, they will pull back. You've just caused that person to engage their opposition reflex.

Now that you know why everything you've tried so far to stop your dog from pulling on the leash hasn't worked, let's move on to what does work.

Building an Outdoor Relationship

The first step to loose-leash walking is building your relationship outdoors. This isn't hard, but it does take some forethought. Your dog must learn that there is "no such thing as a free lunch." After all, we have to work for a living, and the dogs should, too. Note: If you have a dog that isn't obsessive about the environment, then you can skip these next few steps. If however, you have a dog that hits the ground running the instant he goes through the door, then yes, you'll need this!

Before teaching any behavior outdoors, you must build your relationship and get the dog's attention. Follow these steps—hand-feed your dog most of his day's ration of food for behaviors rather than for "free" in his bowl, and "his wish is your command":

1. Take your dog's daily ration of food, mix in some smelly treats, put it in your pockets or pouch, and go outside.

2. Work on eye contact, name recognition, "Sits" and "Downs," and anything else your dog may know how to do at the moment.

3. If your dog is too stimulated by your yard, just wait. Whenever he gives you some kind of attention, instantly reward it.

4. If, after about 10 minutes, he still hasn't noticed that you exist, put him back in the house and in his crate for a several minutes and try again later.

Pointers
If the dog doesn't notice that you exist, ask yourself questions such as, "Are the distractions too much for my dog to handle at this time in his training?" "Did I go from the living room to the football game in one step?" "Was I distracted or not in the mood?" Always set the dog up to succeed and he will!

Continue to do this for a few days—feeding for attention and simple behaviors. Now move to a new location and start all over, waiting patiently for attention and simple behaviors. Every few days, move to a new location and repeat all of the preceding steps. The dog has to know that you aren't a dead tree stump. After about one to two weeks of practicing in about five to seven spots, you'll be ready to start training for loose-leash walking. You must establish "getting and keeping" your dogs attention before moving onto the next steps. Try loose leash walking without it and you'll get tight leash pulling.

Be the "Stupid Bunny"

I compare heeling and loose leash walking to a bunny rabbit. There are two kinds of bunnies:

1. The "smart" bunny, when seeing a predator, freezes. If the prey isn't moving, the predator won't see it. This bunny gets to live another day.

2. The "stupid" bunny, when seeing a predator, runs and hops and zig-zags. That bunny has now attracted the predator and will most likely have a hard time remaining free.

I want you to be the "stupid" bunny! Move erratically, lots of pace and direction changes and your dog will be magically glued to you! Except it isn't magic — it's modern training in action!

I like teaching a "heel" first, and then a loose leash walk. That way, your dog will develop a history of paying attention to you which makes loose leash walking a cinch! Dogs think about what they're looking at, so if they aren't looking at you, then guess what? They aren't thinking about you either. Heel is when your dog is on your left hand side, his head by the seam of your pants as he looks up at you adoringly.

To start out teaching a heel, play is your first step. Why? Because heeling is a team sport and it is important that your dog learns to pay attention to you while you are both moving. With the two of you facing each other, just feint left and right in a very excited manner (like a football player), then click and treat your dog for staying with you. Be very enthusiastic though, otherwise he may not follow you. Practice this in a few locations for a few days.

Alert!
If you have a timid dog, the play might frighten him, so skip the above step for now. Once he develops some confidence, you can go back to it.

Feint right and left and reinforce your dog for following you.

Photos: T. Hirsch

You're going to practice this quite a bit because not only is it the first step of teaching a heel, but it can also become a very strong reinforcer. See chapter 12.

Moving Backups

The second step to teaching heeling is "moving backups."

Follow these steps:

1. After playing for a minute or so, walk backward (walk is the important word here — if you jog backwards, you will trip and hit your head). Click and treat when your dog follows you. You're not looking for eye contact yet. Be sure to back up in wavy lines — straight is boring for most dogs.

2. Don't lure your dog with cookies — have your hands down by your sides or up toward your chest. If he mugs your hands, put them behind your back.

3. Take a few more steps back and click and treat every few steps.

4. Gradually increase the number of steps you back up before clicking and treating. Now you can wait for eye contact before you click and treat. Mix and match between playing ("be the bunny") and backing up.

Walking backward - dog is following you.
Photos: T. Hirsch

If your dog looks away, you can either ...

• Continue to back up and click and treat when he comes back into position.

• Stop moving and wait for the dog to reengage with you (by giving you eye contact); then continue to back up and then click and treat.

Backing up and pivoting so now the dog is on your left in heel position.

Photos: T. Hirsch

Pivot to heel

Once your dog is following you while you're backing up, put the leash and clicker in your right hand and the treats in your left hand. When he is really looking at you, pivot to your right, so the dog is now on your left. Click and treat with your left hand.

After each click and treat, place your left hand up at your tummy. This will become your heel cue — bent left arm. Take a few steps forward and click and treat again. Use a high rate of reinforcement at first and gradually use less and less food for more and more heeling. Why do I ask that you feed with your left hand? Because if your dog is on the left and you feed with your right hand, he will cross in front of you and trip you!

The Art

Don't name this yet, because if you name a sub-standard behavior, that's what you'll get when you ask for it. Wait until it is as perfect as you want it to be and then name it. While in training mode, I use an interim word, such as "let's go." Once you like what you see, you can start to name it your real cue. "Heel," "strut," "with me," and "march" are the most common heel cue words.

Heeling games

Start making heeling fun and very relevant, by adding in turns and halts with automatic sits.

"This way"

As you are about to turn to the right (away from your dog), pause for an instant, say his name and "this way." When he stays with you (on your left) as you turn, click and treat. Because I frequently walk my dogs off leash, they often go into the bushes. If they don't check in right away, I say "this way!" and they all come running because "this way" is now also a change of direction cue.

Automatic sit

To teach an automatic sit, simply lure your dog into a sit (and verbally say "sit") as you are about to stop (not after you stop). Do this a dozen or so times and your dog will automatically sit in heel position when you stop.

Call front

There may come a time when you are presented with something you don't want your dog to engage in—such as a skunk, bear, deer, an aggressive dog or a cat. You need your dog's attention and you need it fast! Practice this in advance and you'll have that instant response when you need it.

As you are heeling, call your dog to you as you back up a few steps and have him sit in front of you. Click and treat. You can also practice grabbing his collar (see chapter 7) in case you get boxed in somewhere.

Follow the Leader

An alternate method to teach heeling is to actually start without a leash. If your dog wants to stay with you without a leash, then adding the leash is a piece of cake. To start this, I like to play "follow the leader" on either a 50-foot-long line or off leash completely in a safe, fenced-in area.

The Art

Occasionally I will work with a dog that just doesn't understand the "be the bunny" game or the walking backwards game, so I will start with follow the leader. I've also run across a few dogs that are afraid of the "be the bunny" game, so we skip it and go to step two. Often, once the dog learns to trust their owner a bit more, we can add in the play. Never fear, there's always another way!

Arm yourself with tons of yummy treats and follow these steps:

1. Give your dog one treat.

2. Walk away. (Don't use any verbal cues or commands with this game. You want your dog to stay with you because he wants to, not because you're forcing him to do so with the leash, or constantly prodding him verbally.)

3. If your dog follows you, feed him treats and pet and praise him for a full 20 seconds.

4. Now change direction. If your dog stays with you, reinforce him again for a full 20 seconds. After each set of reinforcers, change direction.

5. Repeat until your dog stays by your side as you move around.

6. If your dog comes toward you but charges on ahead, turn around and walk away from him. The name of this game is called "follow the leader," and he isn't the leader. You are.

7. Keep repeating until your dog stays with you.

Some dogs are successful with this game within a few minutes and some dogs take hours to stay around their owners. If your dog is one of the few who won't focus on you, please don't be angry. Just backtrack and work on more focus at home first. Look at yourself — are you being the bunny? Are your reinforcers the best they can be?

Loose-Leash Walking

Once your dog is successful heeling, either on or off leash, you can start training a loose leash walk. My definition of loose leash walking is that the dog can be anywhere — in front, on the right or left or even behind — as long as the leash is loose. Above all, remember, the leash is not a tool. It's a safety net!

Try to start this in a low-distraction area. As always, you want to set the dog up for success as much as possible. After all, I bet you didn't learn to drive on a major highway—you probably started in an empty parking lot. Gradually work up to heavy distractions. The higher the distraction level, the higher value your reinforcers should be.

Automatic check-in

Take your dog out for a walk, preferably on at least a 15 foot leash (don't use a retractable lead — they actually encourage dogs to pull because there is always tension on the dog's neck). Your left arm will be straight down, which signals a loose leash walk (if your left arm is bent, that is your non-verbal heel cue). Start this in a boring parking lot.

1. Walk about 200-300 yards. Keep an eagle eye out for your dog's attention. If he looks back to you, squat down (to encourage him to come to you) and have a party! If he pulls you, just walk very very slowly. Sometimes just doing that will get their attention (their look might say, "Hello?! Are you coming?")

2. Repeat this for about 15-20 minutes and you should start to see your dog checking in every minute or so.

Automatic check-in with name/come response

1. Do the same thing as the previous step and this time, when your dog looks back to you, say his name and/or your come cue. Jackpot when he comes!

2. Mix it up — sometimes say nothing and sometimes use his name or his name/come cue, but always jackpot (for a full 20 seconds).

Click the leash, not the dog!

Once you've done all of the above steps, you're ready to now click the leash for being loose and then just toss the dog a treat. Yes, you're not clicking the dog, you'll click the leash.

If you feed in heel position, your dog will go back to heeling. Not a bad thing really, but we are now teaching a loose leash walk. I have found that when the owner is concentrating on their dog, they lose sight of the whole picture and that picture is a loose lead. By using a longer leash, you'll have more time to react and get that click and treat in before the leash gets taut.

It's really that simple. I taught my Border collie Emma (who I think was a sled dog in a previous life) to loose leash walk this way after nothing and I mean nothing worked to stop her from pulling. Her heeling was perfect, but loose leash walking was non-existent. All it took was two 15 minute sessions and the lightbulb went on in her furry brain.

Practice going from heel to loose leash walking to heel and back again. Make it fun!

Does "be a tree" really work?

Maybe. I say maybe because if you do it right (just like with anything else), it works. Do it wrong and it goes south pretty quickly. "Be a tree" is not my favorite method for teaching loose leash walking, but some people may find it effective.

The wrong way: You stop moving when your dog pulls and then reward him right away when he stops pulling. This will only teach him to pull, stop, get a treat. Cha-cha-cha. If this sounds like what you're going through, re-read this chapter.

The right way: You stop moving when your dog pulls, move forward again when he stops pulling and then reward him for walking nicely. You can change direction while he is looking toward you (so as not to jerk his collar), and/or pat your leg to encourage him to stay with you — long enough to reinforce the correct loose leash walking behavior.

Turning Your Worst Distraction into Your Greatest Ally

I can hear you groaning already! Dogs, kids, leaves, planes, cars, bicycles, deer, squirrels, birds, smells of all kinds, cats—the list is endless and frustrating. How can you use these distractions to your benefit? Build a strong positive relationship with your dog and become your dog's benevolent "Higher Power."

You've laid the groundwork by hand-feeding your dog for behaviors for a few weeks and now you have his attention outside. You've been practicing "follow the leader," "heel," and some loose-leash walking in a relatively distraction-free area. You've been practicing your recalls. You're doing a great job!

Once you've built a solid foundation, you can now use the distractions that have driven you crazy to help build your relationship to an even higher level.

Use sniffing as a reward for walking nicely by your side. Follow these steps:

1. Get a few steps of loose-leash walking, (perhaps starting in a parking lot — let's make it easy for the dog to succeed) click and then run over to some grass and while you point to the ground, say, "Go sniff."

2. Let him have a penny's worth of sniffing and then verbally encourage him to come with you, without using the leash to drag him.

3. Heavily reward his recall, even if at first it wasn't all that prompt.

4. Do a few more steps of loose-leash walking and reward again with some sniffing.

Within a few repetitions, you should see your dog start to sniff less and less, and to be interested in you for longer periods of time. Why? Because you've ceased being a barrier to his fun and are now an active partner.

"I'm with you, you're with me" Dance

I love this game and so do my students. With your dog on at least a 15 foot long line, you follow him and stay within two feet of him. If he wants to sniff, you stay with him, if he wants to go that way, you stay with him. Caveat: of course, if he's racing away at top speed after a scent, then no, don't follow him.

After a few minutes of you being with him, change it and cue a heel. Then go back to you being with him and then back to heel again.

By dancing this dance, you'll really build on that relationship — you don't always have to take "charge;" sometimes you can just "be with" your dog. It's truly a liberating experience for both of you!

Pop Quiz

1. If you stop moving when your dog starts to pull, should you reinforce him the instant he comes back to you?

2. If you let your dog pull on leash sometimes and not other times, what is your dog learning?

3. If you yank on the leash when he is pulling, what is your dog learning?

4. Have you started to use other types of reinforcers for loose-leash walking?

5. Have you noticed a positive difference in his attention to you?

Summary

Dogs pull because we follow, because they want to investigate, and because of opposition reflex.

Build your outdoor relationship first before teaching loose-leash walking.

Teach a heel and the heeling games first. Then loose leash walking will be a breeze.

Stop being a barrier to your dog's fun; use what he wants as a reward for walking nicely.

Teaching the Stays 9

The "Stay" behavior is almost as hard to teach as loose-leash walking. We spend much of our time training our dogs to stay close to us and heavily rewarding them for it; now we want them to stay waaaay over there?

The different types of "stays" may be difficult to teach, but are very important, as they can be life-saving for our dogs. They are helpful when you have a multiple-dog household, such as stopping them from getting in your way and tripping you while you're running for the phone.

"Stays" are useful for the vet's office, grooming, toenail clipping, or waiting at the front door, car door, and crate door before releasing them in or out. They're essential for competition obedience, agility, sheep herding, and any other dog sport.

In addition, the stay behavior is great for teaching your dog to "stay on his mat," so that you can eat dinner without being pestered or without the dog begging (and by this point, you understand that all begging behavior is caused by someone feeding the dog from the table, thus reinforcing the dog for begging).

"Sit," "Down," and "Stand Stay"

Obviously, to start teaching the "Stays," you must already have trained the "Sit," "Down," and "Stand" behaviors. Please review Chapter 5 before starting the stay behavior.

Teaching stays are relatively simple and for this behavior alone, I don't use the clicker:

1. Ask your dog to sit

2. Remind him to sit and pivot your upper torso away (keeping your feet planted) and quickly pivot back in and treat.

3. Repeat step two until your dog is solid — usually three to five repetitions

4. Remind him to sit again and this time, start to take a step away, but keep one foot planted; go back in and treat. Repeat three to five times until he's solidly staying, then go onto the next step.

5. Once he is staying nicely, turn away and leave him just one step at a time.

6. Once he's staying nicely, turn away and take another step away.

7. Repeat until the dog stays in position.

You'll notice that I am not asking you to say "stay" yet, because if you name it now and he gets up, you've paired the behavior of "get up" with the word "stay." Wait until it is perfect and for now, just use a reminder cue of "sit." At any time if he breaks the stay, just go back and reposition him and try again. Once you can go approximately 10-15 feet away and he hasn't budged, then you can start adding the word stay. I use "Sit stay" as a transition and then eventually get rid of the "sit" part. For the down as well as the stand, you'll do the same steps as listed above.

The Art
Be sure you turn your back to the dog when you leave. Backing away while chanting "stay, stay, stay" won't work in the long run and doesn't work in real life. Why? Because in real life you'll need to turn away from him to deal with whatever it is you need to do — sweep up broken glass, pick up a pill you dropped, etc., and if you don't practice turning away, then he'll break his stay and possibly get hurt.

If your dog breaks at any point, you must ignore him for about 3-5 seconds and then just reset the session. Make sure the dog won't run out in traffic when you ignore him. Be prudent. Be safe. If all of a sudden your dog breaks his stay a few times in a row, think. He may be tired, thirsty, need to relieve himself or perhaps something in the environment changed to make him nervous.

> **Pointer**
> If you ask your dog to "Sit" and he sits and then goes into a "Down," this does not constitute a "Stay." "Stay" means "stay in that position until I come back and release you." And this is the "art" as well — if it's "good enough" for you, then it's fine with me. However, if it's not really what you want, then don't reinforce it. What you reinforce is what you'll get!

Door Etiquette
Let's say your dog won't sit quietly at the door and charges through each time you open it. You let him do this. Winter comes, your stoop is a sheet of ice, your dog pulls you through the door, and you fall down and hurt yourself. Should you be angry at your dog? Nope! You trained your dog to charge through the door in the first place!

So what should you do? The obvious solution is to teach a "Wait at the door until I release you to go through," also known as "proper door etiquette." Follow these steps for the house and the car doors:

1. Approach a door with the dog.

2. Ask the dog to "Sit" or "Down." (Be sure to train the sit and/or down stay before working in the door context.)

3. Put your hand on the doorknob.

4. If the dog stays in position, reinforce the dog.

5. Then turn the knob without opening the door.

6. If the dog stays in position, reinforce the dog. If he moves, ask him to "Sit" again and don't take your hand off of the doorknob.

7. Repeat until the dog stays in position.

8. Now it's time to actually open the door a tiny bit. If he moves, ask him to "Sit," or you can say "Sit" while you open the door. Reinforce the dog if he doesn't move.

Continue in this manner, opening the door more and more while continuing to reinforce the "Sit" and "Stay" behavior.

When you can successfully go through the door without your dog, (he is still in a stay) you're halfway there! Now it's time to train the second half — when you call him through the doorway, he should come to front position and sit. This will come in handy when there are distractions on the other side of the door. Here's how to get it;

1. Once you go through the door, say your dog's name and come cue.

2. When he comes out and sits in front of you, ask for a "Sit" and reinforce him.

3. Repeat until the dog automatically comes to front position when you call him out of his stay.

You'll notice that I don't want you to use a release cue, such as "okay" or "free" for door etiquette. Why? Because a release cue is just that — a release, and door etiquette isn't a release. It's really a stay and then a recall.

The dog should learn to automatically look back at you after going through any and all doors. If needed, you can also lure the dog to sit in front of you for a few reps until he learns the pattern.

Proper door etiquette coming out of the house and car door.

photos: T. Hirsch

Adding Distractions to the Stay and All Other Behavior

Next up—the dreaded distractions! The list is endless. Kids, bikes, cars, dogs, people, birds, squirrels, deer—you name it, it can be a distraction.

Start out with mild distractions—say, one other person walking slowly around. This person can be a stranger or a friend helping you train. If a friend, have that person walk faster, then jog, then run. Then add another person, and another. You can start to add toys (do not tease the dog with them), perhaps another well-trained dog at a distance, and other types of distractions. Always be sure that you add them one at a time, always set the dog up for success.

> ### *Pointer*
> When you add each new distraction, you must start again at the beginning, depending on what you're working on — be it a sit, down, stand, any of the stays, eye contact, name and come recognition.

Be sure that once you start a higher intensity of distractions you go back to easier steps. If the dog breaks, or doesn't respond, say to yourself, "No big deal, I asked for too much" and just try again. Stay away from any verbal "corrections." Silence works best.

Wait a Minute!

Many people use just one word—"Stay"—to mean a few different things. Some like using two words: "Stay" and "Wait." To me, they have different meanings. "Stay" means "You stay there until I come back to you." "Wait" means "Wait there until I give you another cue." If you feel more comfortable using just one word, that's not a problem as long as you're clear in your direction to your dog. Do what you'll remember and be consistent with it.

Two important uses of the "Stay"and "Wait;" have your dog go to his mat and "Stay" there, and to "Wait" to be released to eat dinner.

Go to Your Mat!

Let's teach your dog to go to his mat. You may not think this is any big deal and that your dog doesn't need to know this, but it's very useful in many scenarios.

If your dog is bugging you and you're busy, you can tell him to go to his "Mat," "Bed," or "Place"—whatever word you want to use. For dogs who have been reinforced for begging at the table, this is great to use. Basically, this is "target training." You're teaching your dog to "target" the mat and lie down on it and stay there.

Follow these steps:

1. Have a mat or bed set up.

2. Sit in a chair about five feet away.

3. Throw cookies onto the mat and don't say anything yet.

4. As the dog steps on the mat, click and throw some more treats.

5. Repeat this about 24 times.

6. If the dog goes back to the mat of his own accord, click and throw treats. (The dog is doing the behavior and is then rewarded, rather than "luring" the dog onto the mat with the treats.)

At this point you still won't say anything to the dog. Get the full behavior (which is "go to your mat and lie down"), and then give it a name. Dogs aren't really listening to us anyway — they do better if we're quiet and let them think.

Now stop throwing cookies onto the mat. Look at your dog. Once he has also engaged your eye contact, look at the mat. Look at his face again and then look at the mat. If he looks at the mat or goes over to the mat, click and throw the treat on the mat. If he doesn't move, look at him again and then stare at the mat. For any movement toward the mat, be it head or body movement, you should click and throw cookies onto the mat. This rewards the dog's attention and orientation to the mat.

1. Once your dog goes to the mat either on his own or with the help of your eye, as he steps on the mat, ask him to lie down.

2. Then click and treat the behavior.

3. Repeat this about 10 times or until he goes to the mat and lies down on his own.

4. Once he's going to the mat and lying down on his own, you can now name it "Go to your mat" as he's lying down. Repeat that at least 10 times.

5. Start to say "go to your mat" before he does it and just wait (and look at the mat). If he goes to the mat and lies down, click and jackpot. If he doesn't, just backtrack.

6. Once your dog goes to the mat on cue on a regular basis, start to add distance — right now you're five feet away, so step back one extra foot at a time, do a few reps, then step back another foot and so on.

Very quickly, your dog will, upon hearing you say, "Go to your mat," go to the mat and lie down. Now you have to build distance, duration, and changing location.

Detail

My dog Cody taught me (without speaking one word of English) that by staring in the direction I want a dog to look, he'll turn his head that way. After I gave each of my dogs a bone, Cody came up to me after about 10 minutes, whining and turning his head repeatedly. I normally ignore him when he whines because I don't want to reinforce whining. However, I did glance at him out of the corner of my eye and realized he was looking at Beau and then back to me. Beau had stolen Cody's bone and he wanted me to get it back for him. Try it sometime—it is just too cool! And you never know, you may just find a use for it someday.

Changing locations is great to work on—move the mat to different parts of the house and yard. Wouldn't it be great to go to a softball game, bring your mat, and ask the dog to go to his mat and he does it! And stays there! And doesn't annoy the other people there! Wow! Your friends will be amazed!

You'll also need to build distance. Let's say you're in the kitchen and the mat is in the living room. Your dog wants attention, but you're talking on the phone, cooking dinner and transferring hot things from the stove to the table—not a good time for your dog to be underfoot. That's a perfect example of a time to tell your dog to go to his mat.

When building distance, be sure to move away from the mat only a few feet at a time. Just as when you were teaching "Stay," building distance slowly is important to the success of the behavior.

Waiting for Dinner

Waiting for dinner may not seem like a behavior you'll need, but it's an excellent and simple way to introduce the word "Wait" into your dog's vocabulary. I like it because it also teaches some self-control to the dog, so that he doesn't get pushy and forceful around food.

Follow these steps:

1. Put a few pieces of food in a bowl on the counter.

2. Ask the dog to "Sit."

3. Start to put the bowl on the floor.

4. If at any time he moves out of position, take the bowl away.

5. Remind the dog to "Sit" again.

6. Repeat steps three and four. Don't add the word "Wait" yet—again,

silence is best. Get the behavior first—then name it. After a few repetitions of steps three and four, you won't even have to remind the dog to "Sit" again—he will most likely fix himself.

7. Once the dog waits for even one second, click and release him to the food bowl.

8. As soon as he waits for three to five seconds, you can say the word "Wait."

9. You can increase the "Wait" time to be as long as you wish.

This easily transfers to "Wait" in the car, in the crate or at the door, all of which may just save his life one day. "Stay" can be boring to teach, but the benefits are enormous, so please don't skimp or rush through training it.

Alert!
Pushiness around food or toys is not acceptable behavior. Many people misinterpret this behavior as being dominant, when in fact it's just the behavior of an untrained, spoiled dog who was probably reinforced (unknowingly of course) in the past for being obnoxious.

The Art
The art is that you have to take it on the road as quickly as possible. Just because your dog knows to "wait for his food bowl in the kitchen," doesn't mean that he will understand it in different places in different contexts.

Pop Quiz

1. If you have built up to 30 seconds of a "Stay" in your living room, how many seconds should you start at each new location?

2. Have you started to work on "Wait" for the food bowl?

3. How far away have you gotten from the mat?

Summary
Take it literally one step at a time and your dog will have a solid stay.

Start out building duration with little or no distraction; then add distance to your "Stays."

Once you have distance and duration, you can add distractions.

Practice "Go to your mat" and "Wait for the food bowl" to build your dog's patience and self-control.

Puppy Socialization 10

Puppies are like little sponges—they soak up whatever you teach them, whether it's what you want or not. It's your job to make sure all of those early associations are good ones. I've worked with many eight-week-old puppies and they very rapidly learn proper behaviors without the use of punishment.

This chapter is devoted to socialization and the things you need to do to make sure your puppy grows into a confident adult. If you don't have time to do these things for your puppy; perhaps you work long hours, or have many family and kid activities, you might want to get an older dog. It's your responsibility to "bring up baby" correctly and humanely.

The optimum time for early socialization is 8 weeks to 20 weeks. Any time after that and you'll be dealing with counterconditioning and desensitization because you've lost your window of opportunity.

Everyone says that you should "properly socialize" your new pup, but no one tells you exactly how to go about it. Because socialization is so vitally important to your dog's future mental and emotional well-being and outlook on life, it's imperative to start your new pup off on the right paw. Please be aware that "early" doesn't mean "only." If you "only" take advantage of early socialization and then think you're done—you're not. Socialization can (and should) start as early as eight weeks and should be a continuing process until the dog is two years of age.

As your puppy gets older, he may develop new fears. One day he'll be fine with something or someone, and the next day he'll be terrified. These are called fear periods. The typical ages for fear periods are 8 to 10 weeks of age, then 16 to 20 weeks, at approximately 6 months of age, and again around 10 months of age. Fear periods return at around 14 to 18 months. Keep in mind that these are normal growth behaviors in young dogs as they mature.

It's vital that you don't laugh at, scold, or comfort the dog during fear periods. Keep them relatively isolated during these times and introduce them to nothing new. They are vulnerable during these fear periods, but if you're taking him to class, that's fine — just go easy on the new stuff for a short time. You'll know when they come back to normal and you can then resume taking them out and about. Ignore and wait for calm behaviors that you can then reinforce. If you pressure a puppy during a fear period, he may have that fear for life. Try to schedule spay and neuter (discuss with your vet) when your dog isn't in a fear period — it may be traumatic for them.

Some people think that socializing a dog means indiscriminately dragging him around to new locations or having strangers walk up and invasively pet your pup. This method of "socialization" often frightens a young dog and may lead to fear or aggression based behavior problems later. Proper socialization is actually a controlled introduction of various situations, people and objects, allowing the dog to develop positive associations with them.

> *Definition*
> Socialization involves the controlled introduction of various situations, people and objects so that the dog has the opportunity to develop positive associations with them.

Socialization is about exposing your puppy and adolescent dog gradually and systematically to different types of people, including well-behaved children, places, things, surfaces, noises, touch (from you and strangers), other dogs, and other species of animals. Socialization is all about setting the dog up for success—introducing him to each new situation in such a manner that he won't be afraid. The goal is to build confidence and trust of you and the world.

Watch Carefully for Signs of Stress

The most important responsibility that you have is to watch for signs of stress and fear in your puppy. If you don't recognize these signs, you may be pushing the dog into a situation that he can't deal with and may be creating more fear, aggression, or anxiety about a specific place/person/species. (See Chapter 3 for the observable signs of stress.) If your dog exhibits any of these signs, this may be an indicator that you have pushed your socialization session too fast or for too long.

Places for Socialization

What will your dog have to feel comfortable with during his lifetime? He'll visit the veterinarian and groomer, where strangers will handle him in sometimes very uncomfortable ways. You'll want to take your dog to the park, new and different places, and in and out of strange doorways. You'll also want him to be comfortable in a crate as well as the boarding kennel. He'll also need to feel comfortable with strangers coming into your house.

Start with short visits when going to the vet and groomer, before you actually need their services. Bring treats and toys, hang out for a little while and go home. Repeat many times. Many vets will also allow you to put your dog up on a table (scary, slippery, high up) and the vet will pet them. Believe me, they'll be thrilled you're taking the time now, because that means less problems for them later on!

The dog will need to feel comfortable walking on different types of surfaces such as concrete, gravel, linoleum, carpet, wood or tile floors, grass, snow, puddles, mud, and ice. You need to build his confidence in going up and down all different types of stairs, jumping into the car or using a ramp on his own (especially useful if you have a large-breed dog), riding quietly in the car, and walking along a busy street. Your dog needs to get used to seeing or hearing men in hats or with beards, people in wheelchairs, kids on skateboards, umbrellas, babies crying, kids playing, bicycles, loud music, blow dryers, clippers, cars, trucks and buses driving by, (and don't forget the UPS truck!) other dogs—the list is endless!

> ### *Alert!*
> We have all experienced children and adults coming up to our dogs and wanting to pet them. In this litigious society, it's important to get in touch with your pet's state of mind when you expose him to others. It's also important to teach strangers, especially overly excited children, the correct way to approach your dog.

To Home School or Not to Home School

You can and should start your puppy in puppy kindergarten as soon as possible. My preference is about eight to nine weeks of age. They still retain immunity from the first set of puppy shots and their minds are wide open to learning new things. You have the added benefit of not letting problems happen in the first place in any number of areas—with dogs, strangers, new sights and sounds, handling, house training, nipping, etc. As with all training classes, be sure to go and observe first before signing up.

Many vets still think that you should keep your puppy under "house arrest" until they are five to six months old. The problem with that is the window for socialization is from eight to 16 or 20 weeks. Once closed, it can never be opened again and you may have a real problem later on. See the Appendix for the link to an article by the American Veterinary Society of Animal Behavior for the correct timing of puppy kindergarten.

Is One Class Enough?

In a word: No! Go to school numerous times! Really, I mean it! The average puppy kindergarten lasts from six to eight weeks. Don't expect your puppy to be thoroughly "socialized" with other dogs for the rest of his life in such a short time. If you know of some puppies that are of the same approximate age and they get along, don't be afraid to create your own puppy play group.

See what the school offers in terms of additional training levels. I personally offer Advanced Puppy K (mostly off leash), Performance Puppy (for those puppies that already have their careers laid out), agility, Rally, tricks, Canine Good Citizen, Therapy Dog and so much more.

Even if you have other dogs at home and your puppy gets along fine with them, don't think this is enough. Your new puppy needs to be exposed to many other dogs in his lifetime. Be sure, however, that the puppies and older dogs you introduce him to are friendly. It would be terrible to have your puppy attacked and possibly traumatized for life, ending up fearful of his own species. Bear in mind that many adult and senior dogs are intolerant of exuberant puppies, and are often not interested in being around them. If the puppy doesn't listen to the elder canine, they often find themselves being rolled, bit, or physically disciplined, creating the scary situation that you so much want to avoid.

How About Dog Parks?

I am not a big fan of dog parks. There may be some groups out there that "interview" the dogs to make sure they are safe and will be a nice playmate for your puppy or older dog, but that isn't the norm. Dog parks are usually open to the public, meaning anyone with any dog at any time, can enter. Most people do not possess the ability to properly recognize if their dog gets along with other dogs, or when their dog is over stimulated and not appropriate for that kind of situation. I hear stories about people bringing their dog aggressive dog to dog parks, erroneously thinking that is the best place to "socialize" their dog! Yikes! Many dogs get hurt and killed every year at dog parks. There is no legal recourse for the owners, as all liability is checked at the gate.

If you really feel like you must go to a dog park, then research it; go and watch first — without your dog/puppy to see how the play looks to you. See if the site is broken down into separate little, medium and big dog yards, and observe how the dogs in each group play. You wouldn't want to bring your Maltese puppy into a group of Labs and Goldens who all play rough. Also keep in mind that even if you come across a group that is playing nicely, your dog would be the "newbie," and not necessarily warmly welcomed by that group of dogs. Dogs are by nature territorial and given to intruder alert, which your dog would be to an established group.

Strangers

Many puppies are friendly by nature, but not all. If your pup is a bit hesitant with strangers, start by allowing your dog to observe strangers from a distance. Let him get closer and let him do the approaching. He might be nervous if strangers come up to him. You can have the person feed treats or you can feed treats. That way, positive associations are happening while strangers approach (there's Pavlov again!). If John Q. Public starts to stress your dog out, you can just lure him away with a treat at the earliest signs of stress you see. If you've done your homework, your dog won't be nervous when strangers lean over him.

Go to a place where there are just a few people and few distractions, staying approximately 50 to 100 feet away. As the dog continues to remain calm, remember to reinforce that behavior before moving in closer.

If your dog is frightened and tries to back up or run away, let him move away until he's comfortable. He'll let you know when he's ready to re-approach. Allow the dog to set the pace.

Alert!

It's easy to get caught in the trap of thinking that if your dog is frantically wagging his tail, then he's deliriously happy. A frantically wagging tail is just that—frantic. (Yes, even if your puppy is a Lab.) It's a typical submissive behavior, showing stress. It's one way that a subordinate puppy approaches an adult dog. He's saying, "Please don't kill me, I am so cute!"

If you push your dog and he is frightened and growls, lunges, or barks, do not verbally or physically reprimand him. Why? By punishing him, he'll make the association that "when people are around, bad things happen." Do this enough and he will become a fearful, aggressive dog that will bite people in the future.

Keep your sessions short—just a few minutes each time. Go to as many different locations as you can, as often as you can.

Alert!

Please don't skimp or try to rush ahead with socialization. Your patience will be rewarded.

The Environment

When introducing your dog to "stuff," be sure to do it gradually. After all, drainpipes can be scary! The best way to handle introductions is to be passive and ignore all but calm reactions to things. If the dog is terrified of a piece of paper, don't laugh, don't comfort, and don't scold. Just stand there quietly—you can laugh hysterically later— and then reinforce calm behavior.

Go through your list of "things my dog needs to get used to" systematically and carefully, and you will have a nice, well-grounded puppy who grows up into a nice, well-adjusted adult.

Doggie Food Bowls

I personally never bother my dogs when they're eating, just as I don't encourage them to bother me when I'm eating. Some people think that they should (and must) be able to stick their hands in the bowl while the dog is eating. If you really think it's important, here are the instructions. If you don't train your dog to be calm around food bowls, you may be asking for food-guarding issues later on. Skip these exercises and you'd better fill up your first-aid kit!

Follow these steps:

1. Hand your dog a bowl with a few pieces of food in it.

2. When he's done eating, take the bowl away and give him another one with a few pieces of food in it.

3. Repeat bunches of times — 15 to 20 times.

Now comes the second step:

1. Hand your dog a bowl with a few pieces of food in it.

2. Before he's done eating, slowly lower your hand to the bowl and add more food to it.

3. Repeat 20 to 25 times over the course of a few days.

Third step:

1. Hand your dog a bowl with a few pieces of food in it.

2. Before he's done eating, gently remove the food bowl *at the exact same time* that you hand him another bowl with a few pieces of food in it.

3. Repeat these steps 30 to 50 times over the course of a few days.

Make it fun for your dog — make it more reinforcing when you take the food bowl away than when he keeps it to himself. You can always add more food in the second bowl than you did in the first bowl.

Crate Training

Teaching your dog to love his crate is one of the best things you can do for your new best friend. Your dog will have to be crated many times in his life — for grooming, vet visits, boarding, staying in a hotel or friend's house, in the car, or maybe during a raucous party or if he ever gets lost and is picked up by animal control.

Crate training is essential for younger dogs or rescue dogs to help them not to soil or eat the house. If you don't want your dog jumping in bed with you at 2 a.m. to get you to play, you'll need to put him in the crate. You can also crate your young pup when company comes until you can train him not to jump on visitors or if you wish to go out to dinner. Crates serve as supervision when you're not able to have eyes-on.

Personal Pointers From Pam

If your dog does get lost, there are a few things you can do to ensure that your dog comes home safe and sound.

Microchips: Your veterinarian can insert a small microchip in the shoulder-blade area. Most veterinarians, rescue groups, and shelters have a scanner and can scan the dog to retrieve your contact information. Some animal control agencies also provide this service at a low cost. Don't forget to register the chip number to your name and contact information! Hundreds of animals are picked up every year that are chipped but were never registered, and thus cannot be reunited with their owners.

Embroidered collar: Tags can rip off and if the person who finds your dog doesn't know anything about microchips, etc., at least they'll have your phone number! That happened to me when Emma was 12 years old. She couldn't hear me, was disoriented, ended up in a neighbor's yard. They picked her up (she still had her leash on), but didn't know where she came from and even though all of my dogs are "chipped," they had never heard of a micro-chip. The very next day, I ordered embroidered collars for all of my dogs!

Photos: Always have a current photo on hand in case you need to put up flyers. Be sure to put up a big poster in front of your home.

Emergency info: When you are traveling with the dog, keep information in the car or your wallet in case you have an accident. Include contact numbers of friends who will take the dog, name of veterinarian, any medical information needed, and any behavioral issues the dog may have. Personally I also have this info on my refrigerator and zip-tied to each crate in my van.

Alert!

Martha brought her German Shepherd Nemo to class. One of her complaints was that the dog was chewing up everything in the house. When I recommended crate training, she told me that her husband flatly refused to crate train the dog because "he wants the dog to learn not to chew furniture."

He was under the incredible misconception that Nemo wouldn't chew if he viewed the house and all its contents as his own. After all, when her husband came home and beat the dog for chewing, "it was obvious to the man that Nemo knew what he did wrong." Hello?!?

The Benefits of Crate Training

The benefits of crate training (to both you and the dog) are numerous:

- Makes housetraining easier—be it house soiling or chewing.

- Gives the dog a safe, secure place to "get away from it all."

- Manages the dog when you are busy and can't pay attention to him. This includes when visitors come, when you're leaving for work, when you're cooking dinner and the dog wants to play, and so on.

- Helps you manage a multiple-dog household. For example, I feed my dogs in their crates - that way no one is stealing another dog's food. I also have a strict rule that each time I get a new dog, they have to sleep in their crate in my bedroom for the first two weeks. That way, there's no chance of a tiff and I won't get woken up out of a sound sleep.

- Enables your dog to cope with vet and groomer visits, where he will be crated.

- Makes traveling with your dog easier, safer, and less stressful for both of you.

- Some states have laws now that the dog must be restrained in your vehicle with a crate or seatbelt.

Alert!
When I was a groomer, two Huskies came in for grooming and were not crate trained. One of them was so frantic that she bent the metal bars on the crate door with her teeth and was throwing up bile and blood. Needless to say, I called the owner to come get the dogs, and the dogs didn't get groomed.

Crate-Training Instructions

Break up crate training into several different sessions. Before you start the first session, have lots of treats on hand (my definition of "lots" is about three baggies filled with pea-size treats). Keep the door open and follow these steps:

1. Throw a handful of treats into the crate.

2. Stand back (so as not to pressure the dog) and let him go into the crate on his own.

3. Once he is done eating the treats, throw in more.

Pretty soon, the dog will just stay in the crate, waiting for you to throw in more treats. This usually takes about 10 to 15 minutes.

Alert!
If you do your research well, you can find a breeder who actually crate trains all of the puppies before they leave the nest.

In the next session, throw in a few cookies to "review," and then wait for the dog to go into the crate on his own. Then throw in wads of cookies as a reward (as opposed to a lure) for going into the crate. Then follow these steps:

1. Call him out of the crate and then look at the crate (don't say anything yet).

2. Once he goes back into the crate, reward him again heavily.

3. Repeat the preceding two steps five or six times.

In your third session, follow these steps:

1. Go over to the crate and look at it (still don't say anything).

2. When he goes back into the crate, reward him heavily.

3. Repeat this four or five times.

4. Then, as he is going into the crate (reminder — pair the word with the behavior), say "Crate" or "Place" or whatever you want your word to be for telling the dog to go to his crate.

5. Reward heavily when he goes into the crate.

6. Repeat about five times.

In your fourth session, repeat steps 1, 2, 4 and 5 from the preceding list. Then say the word "Crate" before he goes in, to see if he understands. If he goes into the crate, give him a mega jackpot of treats! Repeat this four to five times and then end the session.

At the fifth session, you'll start closing the door while the dog is comfortable going into his crate. Close the door for about five seconds, while he is still eating the last jackpot you gave him. Before he is done eating, open the door. Let him come out of the crate. Repeat a few times.

In later sessions, start gradually—and I mean gradually (a few extra seconds at a time; use a timer to keep you on track)—keeping the door closed for longer periods of time. You can even sit next to the crate while dropping food into it.

The Art
You must keep this slow. If at any time the dog whines, you have gone on too long. If the dog whines or barks, you cannot let him out of the crate until he is quiet. If you let the dog out of the crate while he is whining, he will learn to whine in his crate—a mega no-no!

You can also use a special toy that he gets only while in his crate. I like frozen Kong toys stuffed with nut butter or other gushy foods, or a marrow bone to keep them occupied. Continue to build up the duration that your dog can stay in the crate to at least a full minute before you start to leave the room.

Follow these steps:

1. Start by doing this for one second. Leave the room and instantly come back.

2. Reward the dog for being quiet.

3. Then leave for two seconds, then three, then four, and so on, always setting the dog up to not whine.

> **Alert!**
> Never, never use the crate as punishment. If your dog is being "bad," put him in his crate, but do it gently and unemotionally and give him a treat anyway. Putting him away after he has been "bad" teaches the dog nothing, but it keeps you from killing him!

The Art
You can also feed the dog his dinner in the crate, which will speed along his acclimation to it. Repeat all of the preceding steps until you can leave your dog in his crate for hours at a time. This will not take as long as it sounds. I crate trained one dog, whom the owner said couldn't be crate trained, in 45 minutes.

The Bathroom Is Outside
Above all, know that housetraining is a human issue, not a dog issue. We are the ones who want and need the dog to use the outside latrine. They don't care at all. It is imperative to give the dog a great deal of access to the outside. If a dog is left alone in the house for long periods of time, you have in essence, denied access to a bathroom and he will have no choice but to eliminate inside.

Have patience with your dog. You wouldn't yell at your child for soiling his or her diaper, so don't yell at your dog. Yelling might make you feel better, but think what association you are creating: squatting around you is dangerous. Forget about "catching him in the act." Just ignore it and resolve to be more attentive to your dog's needs.

Knowing When to Go
Note how soon after eating, sleeping, napping, playing, and drinking your puppy usually needs to urinate and defecate. If, for example, he messes five minutes after eating, then take him outside three minutes after eating.

Learn your dog's signs that he has to go. He is not some little kid who can cram his fists into his crotch, bend his knees, and look desperate. Common signs of "I gotta go!" are intense sniffing, circling, whining, frantic look on his face, bent tail, hunched butt area, enlarged anus. If you are playing with him when you see any of these signs, immediately stop playing and take him out; otherwise, you're asking for a puddle. And it's not the puppy's fault!

> **Pointers**
> Humans have opposable thumbs that can open doors. Dogs do not. Ergo, dogs cannot open doors. So, get up and take the dog out!

Teach your dog to go to the door when he needs to go. As you cross the threshold, say "Outside." Do this for a few weeks. Then when you think he has to go, ask him "Outside?" and he will probably go to the door.

I also find that some dogs like to ring a bell to let you know that they want to go out. For some reason I have yet to figure out, toy dogs will learn faster this way that the bathroom is outside.

- Hang a bell on a string at nose level from the doorknob.

- Put a tiny dab of peanut butter on the bell and encourage your dog to lick it (causing the bell to ring). Click and treat when they do and instantly say "Outside" and take the dog outside.

- Repeat a bunch of times until the peanut butter is gone and they are still ringing the bell and you are still taking them outside.

Most dogs learn this within a few minutes—ring the bell = go outside.

Heavily reward the dog outside when he does his business and in the same spot where he went. The reward doesn't have to be food — praise works well. Do not reinforce him after you're back in the house unless you want him to mess the house. When you can't be watching him, put him in a crate (my recommendation), in an exercise pen, or on an easily cleanable floor. If he does mess on carpeting, be sure to clean it instantly and thoroughly. Otherwise, that spot will forever smell like the bathroom to him.

> **Alert!**
> There are some dogs who may lie—they will ring the bell to let you think they have to go outside, but they really don't need to go. A great way to handle this is to say, "I'll be right there, honey!" Then wait a few seconds. If the dog ends up doing something else, you'll know that he didn't really need to go. If he continues to hang out by the door, then you know that he wasn't lying.

If you can't seem to read your dog's signs, tether him to you with a six-foot leash. This will force you to pay closer attention to him, and you'll be able to get him out faster, with fewer accidents. Another advantage of tethering to you is that the dog can't wander off to eliminate in another room which you get the pleasure of finding later, long after the fact.

False Alarms and Accidents

There may be times when you take your dog out and he won't do his business. Then he comes back into the house and messes at your feet. Please don't get angry with him, it's just counterproductive. The next time you take him out, wait longer until he goes. If it takes 10 minutes, it takes 10 minutes. Ignore the dog, do not engage in play or talk. Bring a book, call your mother, or practice the multiplication tables in your head, but do not bring that dog back into the house until he is empty.

If after 15 minutes he still hasn't gone, put him in his crate, wait for 10 minutes, and try again. Continue to do this until he goes outside. Reward him when he finally does go. You can also try a longer leash — some dogs are "shy" about going so close to another being.

If he does mess the house, grab the nearest newspaper, roll it up, and hit yourself over the head while chanting, "I forgot to watch my dog, I forgot to watch my dog." If your dog laughs, praise him.

Play Time

Play with other dogs is good for your dog. Play time allows your dog to physically exercise and practice canine social and communication skills. Just like children, dogs can play too much and get too tired, cranky or start fighting. What is normal dog play? Just about anything goes: body slamming, biting, mounting, growling, chasing, rearing, wrestling and barking. Different dogs and different breeds of dogs all have many different play styles. The most important thing to remember is that "dogs don't play Parcheesi."

Try to have two dogs of equal size, temperament and age play together. Play between puppies and adult dogs should be supervised at all times, so that the adult dog doesn't act too pushy over the pup and scare or hurt him. Dogs that play well are dogs that go easily between "predator" and "prey" with ease (I chase you/you chase me exchange). At the first signs of stress in your dog, stop the action by walking or standing between the two dogs, and either give your dog a break or leave the area.

If the dogs actually get into a fight, you might need to break it up with assistance of the other dog owner. Grab each dog at the same time by their tails, waist or back legs. DO NOT grab their collars – otherwise you risk a really good chance of getting bit yourself. Take them at least 20-30 feet away from each other, put them back on leash so they can't immediately re-engage, and let things cool down. Then reinforce both dogs once they are calm.

If you see or sense that there may be a tiff (before it happens), you can also "feed the chickens" by scattering handfuls of food on the ground to redirect and calm them. If all is going well, you can lure them away from each other and then let them go back and play later. The proviso is if either dog is aggressive around food...don't do this.

For nipping and jumping issues, see chapters 11 & 15.

Pop Quiz
1. What are the typical ages that dogs go through fear periods?

2. While your dog is in a fear period, what is the best thing to do—socialize him more or keep him relatively isolated in familiar and comfortable situations?

3. How does your dog react around food or bones?

4. Does your dog accept petting willingly or does he avoid your hand as it reaches out?

Summary
Socialization is a controlled introduction to various situations and things so that the dog develops positive associations with them.

Work on the basics from the day you get your pup: petting, handling, people, children food, and food bowls.

Be sure to watch for any signs of stress. If you spot them, stop training and rethink your next session.

One puppy kindergarten does not make a well-socialized or trained dog—continue training!

Self - Control Games $\quad$ 11

As we all know, self control is hard! Bad habits can grow like weeds if you're not observant or pro-active. This chapter will discuss a few different ways to teach your dog self-control.

The two toy game

This is a wonderful game that teaches the dog four very important things:

- Fetch
- Come
- Give
- Don't be possessive about objects. An added benefit is that this is another relationship building game and gives the dog some aerobic exercise. The two toys are important because with two, you and the dog are not always engaging in a prey ownership negotiation.

1. Have two toys of equal value to the dog (identical works best)

2. You stand in the middle of the yard.

3. Throw one toy to the right, telling the dog to "Get it."

4. When the dog gets the toy, encourage him to come to you. If you need to, wave the other toy you have. As he is on his way to you, say "Come."

5. Tease him with the other toy in your hand. When he drops his toy (not before – get the behavior, then give it a name), say "Give" and then instantly throw your toy to the left. Pick up the dropped toy when the dog goes to get the newly tossed one.

Repeat steps 2-5.

Be careful to end the game before the dog gets tired. In the beginning, only throw the toy a few times. Leave him wanting more! You will build desire, not only for the game, but for you as well. Do not take anything forcibly from your dog unless it will instantly kill him. Dogs whose owners constantly battle for whatever is in their mouths, will often become reluctant to come near or become aggressive after they steal something. If your dog has something in his mouth that you don't want him to have, offer a trade with something of equal or better value. If he has a tissue, offer him steak. If for some strange reason he prefers the tissue, let him have it – it won't kill him!

Building toy drive

If your dog doesn't naturally like toys, you can build a desire for them. After awhile, food may pale. To effectively train your dog and keep him from getting bored, you want as many different types of reinforcers at your disposal, so toy drive can be useful. (See also Chapter 12)

Get a tennis ball, slather it in peanut butter and stick in an old sock. Let the dog sniff it. If he becomes interested, let him continue to sniff for a few seconds and then take it away. Next session, repeat. Next session, let him sniff it for a bit longer. Build on this until he goes wild when you bring it out. Gradually let him have it longer and chew on it. Trade for it WHILE he is still interested in it. Gradually decrease the amount of peanut butter on the ball and let him have it for longer and longer periods of time. Tease the dog with it when you are putting it away.

The Art

There is an art to building drive and the key is not to over do it. Picture a triangle with the top point as being the point of no return. You want to get your dog's energy level and desire for the game to build to almost the top, and then stop the game. If you reach the pinnacle of the triangle, the next instant he will already be on the downward slope.

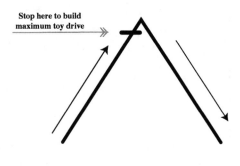

Stop here to build maximum toy drive

At each step of the game, while building drive, the height of that triangle will grow taller (or shorter if you go on too long). Observing your dog will help you with knowing exactly when to stop.

Start to toss it and race with him as he's going toward it. Heavily praise him when he gets it. You can also use "food toys" that look like regular toys but have pockets for treats. When he picks it up, you can then open it and let him eat the treats out of the pocket (or you can hand him the treats).

Make it fun and exciting and you'll have a whole host of additional reinforcers at your disposal!

Tug of war

This is a wonderful relationship builder! Many people have said you should never play tug with your dog because it will make him aggressive. The game doesn't make the dog a predator – he already is one! The game is an outlet. Tug, or any vigorous activity for that matter, played without rules or functioning human brain cells is potentially dangerous. Tug is great because it is intense, increases dog focus and confidence and plugs into something deep inside the dog. The big payoff is in lowered incidence of behavior problems due to under stimulation. And it can be used as a convenient reward for training. You'll notice that your dog will begin to offer you your end of the toy back because the game isn't about winning the toy, it's about the interaction between you and your dog.

As with all games, it must have rules:

You decide when, where, what and how to initiate the game.

Practice the two toy game first, so you have a good "give" cue.

Be alert for signs of the dog being overwhelmed by the game. If your dog starts to growl loudly, re-bite multiple times or looks frantic, you may be over stressing your dog. Stop the game! Just drop your end of the tug and walk away.

If the dog refuses to drop the tug, just walk away.

I let the dog win 100% of the time. This doesn't establish "dominance" in your dog over you, it just builds his confidence.

If your dog takes the toy again before your "take it" cue, tell him to "give."

If he doesn't, even with you waving the second toy at him, drop the toy and end the game by simply walking away.

Intersperse training within the game – ask for a sit, down, heel, whatever, then as a reward, click and tell him to "take it." This will help you start to insert reinforcers other than just food and goes hand in hand with the next game.

Rev up and cool down

I love this game on so many levels.

- It teaches your dog to watch your body language (and vice versa).
- It teaches them to have an "off" switch.
- It teaches him to switch gears (which is also helpful for a recall).
- It also helps with dogs that play nip or jump.

This game is exactly what it says — rev up and cool down. Excite your dog by running around. Before he gets a little too aroused, walk painfully slowly until he matches his pace to yours. Then click and toss a treat on the ground. Repeat as much as you like! In the beginning, you may have a dog that will rev up in one step — zero to 100 in less than one second. That's fine — just take a single running step and go right into walking very slowly. Be sure to match your breathing with your walking — nice long breaths. Gradually increase your "revving," but always watch your dog for signs of over-arousal. Try to time the "cool down" to just before he's over the top.

If you want to, you can name the cooling down behavior. Once the dog is back to walking calmly, use whatever cue word you'll remember. "Easy," "enough," "chill," are all common words to use. This game also helps when you add in behaviors — rev, rev, rev, sit, down, stand, heel, rev, rev, etc. Throw in whatever behaviors you'd like to. Most dogs really get into the spirit of the game and seem to enjoy it as much as you will.

"Mine" a.k.a. Leave it

This exercise is the be-all and end-all of distraction and self-control training! Training a solid "Mine" will help you in real life situations for anything you don't want your dog to interact with — be it another dog, person, goose poo, puddles, carcasses, a dropped pill or dropped food — anything.

I like to use the word "Mine" because so many people have poisoned the words "Leave it" or trained it improperly (such as saying "Leave it" and yanking the dog away) or not at all but still use the words.

A solid "Mine" cue (my positive version of "Leave it") is broken down into 15 easy to understand steps. You may think the exercise would take forever to train—it doesn't. It should take you only two to three weeks, depending on how much you practice, and the time will be well spent, considering the value of the training.

Your basic approach here is that you will make it great fun for your dog to come away from "stuff." For the first two steps only, you will be dropping the food on the floor to take your dog's focus off your hand. From step three on, you will be handing him the treat.

1. Put a treat in your fist and present it to your dog (letting him mug your hand). The instant he moves his head or body away, click and treat, dropping the treat on the ground. Repeat that step until, upon seeing your hand, he is actively moving or looking away and has completely stopped mugging it.

2. Present your closed fist and when your dog backs away, open your hand.

If he doesn't make a move for it, click and treat, dropping the tr... ...
the ground. If he does move toward your hand don't move it away, just
close your fingers. Once he backs away again, open your hand. Continue
to open and close for as long as it takes to get him to move away from
your open hand; then drop the treat on the floor.

From step three onward, you will not drop the food on the ground anymore. Instead,
you will place all of the treats directly into his mouth. This training is valuable in real
life because if you happen to drop something poisonous, your dog won't dive bomb
it and you won't end up at the emergency vet's.

3. Place the treat on the floor and cover it with your hand. When your dog
   stops mugging your hand, click and pick up the treat and put it in his
   mouth. Repeat until he is actively not going toward your open hand.

4. Do the same as step three except now hold your hand slightly away
   from the treat. The goal of this step is to have your dog back away from
   the "naked cookie." Click and pick up the treat and put it in his mouth.
   Repeat this step until you can get your hand farther and farther away
   from the treat without your dog charging it. Once you can put the treat
   down and take your hand away completely, go to step five.

5. You now want your dog to look at your face (you may have to prompt a
   bit — whisper, or a kissie noise) and away from the naked cookie. Click
   when he looks at you, and pick up the treat and put it in his mouth. After
   about 10 repetitions, get rid of the prompting and wait until he looks at
   your face, then click and treat.

6. You can name this now. As he looks at your face, say "Mine," click and
   treat. Practice this about 10-15 times.

7. Step seven is almost identical to step six, except now *as* you place the
   treat on the ground, you'll say "Mine" and click and treat when your dog
   looks at you.

8. This step takes a bit of coordination. Kneel on the ground. Have a treat in
   each hand. Hold one arm out to the side and drop the treat on the floor,
   say "Mine" and at the exact same moment, give him the treat from your
   other hand. Then say "Stay" and pick up the one you dropped and hand
   it to him (you don't need to click for this one unless you have a second
   trainer helping you). Don't block him if he charges for the one you
   dropped (although you can block him with the other treat) and don't say
   anything. Just try again. Repeat this step until he is very much holding position.

Alert!
Why shouldn't you block your dog? Blocking doesn't teach him any self-control. Dogs are very smart—they know when we can block and when we can't, and they will take advantage of every opportunity offered. Don't forget, they are scavengers by nature.

Of course, in real life, if there's something that will kill him or make him sick, use some sense and yes, block him!

9. Now you want a longer stay before you give the dog the treat from your hand. Count to one and then give him the treat, then count to two, and so on.

10 and 11. These two steps are almost identical to step 8 and 9, except you are now standing up (you are now farther away from protecting the dropped treat).

12. Drop the treat with your outstretched hand and call your dog away from it as you back away from the one you dropped. You can cheat the first few times and show him the huge wad of food you have, luring him to you as you say in a happy voice, "Mine! Come!" Again, never block the dog—if he races to the one you dropped, just go back and repeat steps 7 and 8 some more.

13. Place a few empty food bowls in a straight line. Heel your dog past them. Start at a far distance and heavily reinforce him each time you successfully pass a bowl. Gradually get closer and closer, making sure your reinforcers are really good ones. You can say "Mine" as you are going past each bowl, before he may charge over to it. At this stage of the game, saying the cue "Mine" after his face is stuck in the bowl would be setting him up to fail. Be sure that you click and reinforce him for looking away from the bowl—you may have to be really quick in your timing and reinforce him for even a split second of attention.

14. The next step is to have food in one of the bowls and repeat step 13, then food in two of the bowls, and so on, until all of the bowls have food in them. Start with boring dry kibble in the bowls while you have the "big guns" steak, liver, cheese — whatever your dog loves most in the world.

15. Along with the filled food bowls, start to put other things out on the floor — toys, staplers, books, bottles — anything that might draw your dog's interest, and heel around them, saying "Mine" before he goes to investigate.

16. Start to take this "on the road." Go to a place you normally walk and

pepper the walk with stuff — food, toys, anything. Then go back and get your dog. You'll know where everything is, so you'll be able to be pro-active when telling your dog "Mine!"

Summary

Play tug with rules!

Build a desire for toys to add to your reinforcement repertoire

Rev up and cool down will also help to teach your dog self-control

Slots, Soda and Hawaii: Reinforcements 12

Behaviorist B.F. Skinner discovered three reinforcement schedules for animal training. Two of them will create a bored, lazy, and noncompliant dog. Use only those two and you may hear your dog say, "Yeah, sure, when I feel like it." But if you use variable schedule of reinforcement, you'll be sure to get "Sure! When? Yesterday? No problemo!" Add surprise elements and there is no limit to what you and your dog can accomplish.

It's a Shell Game: Different Reinforcement Schedules

B.F. Skinner was the first to discover how variable reinforcement schedules can increase or decrease specific behaviors. Skinner came upon this marvel of observable fact when he was running out of rat-food pellets while performing experiments and the rats still performed the behaviors, at a stable rate, for less food. Wahoo!

Skinner named it "schedules of reinforcement," and the concept opened up a whole new area of study for him and others in behavioral psychology. There are three different types of reinforcement schedules that can be used for training: continuous, fixed, and variable. Some are more effective than others in maintaining or advancing behaviors. Some actually kill behaviors. The technique of utilizing schedules of reinforcement spread to marine mammal trainers and then to dog trainers (and sometimes even to human trainers).

Continuous Reinforcement

Continuous reinforcement was the original method that Skinner practiced, meaning that for every correct behavior, a treat was delivered. This schedule is great for teaching new behaviors.

You can see continuous schedules of reinforcement in your daily life. When you first learned to use a vending machine, it was very reinforcing to put your money in and get a prize. This encouraged you to do it again when you wanted something to eat or drink.

Fixed Schedule of Reinforcement Slows Down Learning

There are two types of fixed schedules: fixed interval and fixed ratio. With a fixed-interval schedule, the food is fed at specific times, rather than for specific behaviors. If your dog does one "Sit" in a 20-second period, he gets one treat. If he doesn't sit, he doesn't get a treat. But even if he sits 100 times in 20 seconds, he still gets one treat. But in this case, something interesting happens; the dog will pace himself by slowing down the rate of his behavior right after the reinforcer, and speed up again when the time for it gets close. Just like some employees at the work place on Monday and then on Friday!

> **Alert!**
> Stick to a fixed-interval schedule and you'll get what's called "scalloping." Say you're having the dog heel and you give him a treat every five seconds (because we humans are creatures of habit). The dog may, after taking the treat, go off and sniff, and then run back after three or four seconds to get his next "fix."

Example: You call your dog from the backyard to no avail. You call at 10 a.m., you call at noon, and you call at 3 p.m. No doggie. However, at 5 p.m., you call your dog and he comes flying. Why? Because you always feed him his dinner at 5 p.m. He knows that no reinforcement is coming at those other times, so he doesn't come when called.

Another type of fixed schedule is the fixed-ratio schedule, which reinforces the dog after so many behaviors on a regular schedule. The dog sits 3, 6, or 20 times and always gets a cookie after the third, sixth, or twentieth time. The number of behaviors asked for remains the same between reinforcers in a fixed-ratio schedule.

Fixed-interval and fixed-ratio schedules can kill behaviors in dogs as well as humans. Fixed ratios are predictable, and predictability is boring, tedious, dreary, and mind numbing.

Okay, so you get the point on how predictability kills behavior. What's the answer? Variable reinforcement, of course!

> **Pointers**
> Because they're predictable, fixed-interval and fixed-ratio schedules can create boredom and dullness in your dog and an overall unwillingness to perform.

Eenie, Meenie, Minie, Mo: Variable Reinforcement

Skinner also looked at two different types of variable reinforcement schedules:

> **Alert!**
> Before you bet 10 dollars that your dog will do any behavior you ask for, you need to move from continuous reinforcement (treating for every correct performance of the behavior) to a variable schedule of reinforcement. After the first 10 sits or so, stop reinforcing for each one. Otherwise, your dog will sit only if you have a treat in your hand. Contrary to what you might think, giving your dog a treat every time doesn't make for strong and reliable behaviors.

variable ratio and variable interval. A variable ratio means that you change the number of behaviors needed each time. First it takes 3 "Sits" to get a treat, then 10, then 1, then 7, and so on.

Variable interval means that you keep changing the time period between reinforcements—first 20 seconds, then 5, then 35, then 10, and so on. As a result, dogs no longer pace themselves, because they can no longer establish a rhythm between behavior and reward.

> ***Definition***
> Behavior extinction occurs when a behavior ceases, usually due to it no longer being reinforced.

Both variable ratio and variable interval keeps dogs on their toes. But most importantly, these schedules are very resistant to behavior extinction. It makes sense if you think about it. In the dog's mind, if he hasn't gotten a reinforcer for a while, well, it might come if he does one more "Sit!"

When the Soda Machine Suddenly Becomes a Slot Machine

When you put money in a slot machine, you know ahead of time that you might not win very often, nor will you know how much the machine will pay out—it could be 25 cents or $500. But...you just might win the very next time, and if you don't try one more time, you might possibly miss on the score of the century!

This is just the opposite of how a vending machine works. You put your money in and a soda comes out. So what happens if you put your money in and nothing comes out? There are a few options you might consider:

- Walk away

- Put in more money and try one more time

- Find a sledgehammer and beat it to death

Now, look at this from your dog's point of view. If you get stuck on a continuous reinforcement schedule and all of a sudden you try to be more variable, your dog's possible reactions could include the following:

- Walk away

- Try to sit again, just to make sure the cookie machine isn't broken

- Bark, whine, or bite in frustration because the cookie machine isn't paying out

Eureka! Variable Reinforcement

In the days before prepackaged rat food, Skinner noticed that he would run low in the middle of an experiment. Because he had to make his own food, he decided that he would reduce the number of reinforcements given for a particular behavior. Skinner discovered that the rats continued to perform their behaviors at a consistent rate.

Behold the discovery of schedules of reinforcement!

Using and understanding variable reinforcement schedules are vital in teaching longer and stronger behavior patterns. Gambling casinos know this, which is why they make so much money on slot machines. Think they just made up the idea of slot machines? Think again! They have scientifically determined the optimum reward schedule—they let you win just enough to keep you hooked! Brilliant!

Variety: The Spice of Your Dog's Life

Add reinforcement variety to variable reinforcement schedules (interval or ratio) and you're home free for life! Variable reinforcement with reinforcement variety is the strongest schedule for maintaining any behavior.

Variety is just that—variety of reinforcement type. The key is not to use the same old thing to reinforce the dog. Reinforcement variety not only makes strong behaviors, but it also helps enrich the dog's life. Here are some examples of reinforcers you can use:

- **Food:** chicken, cheese, hot dogs, liverwurst, tortellini, steak, chickpeas, kidney beans, liver brownies, kibble, burnt leftovers that no one wants, pizza crust, meat scraps, vegetables, fruit; the list is endless.

- **Toys:** tennis balls, Frisbees, tug toys, Kongs (a Kong is a hard rubber toy with a big hole in it that can be tossed or can be stuffed with yummy treats); anything your dog likes to play with. (Exception: Don't use old shoes or socks as toys because the dog will get the idea that your new socks and shoes are also toys.)

- **Activities:** swimming, car rides, walks in the woods, tag-you're-it, chasing you, jogging, hiking, grooming (some dogs do like being groomed), playing with other dogs.

- **"Life rewards":** sniffing that pile of poop, rolling in smelly things, playing with sticks, peeing on bushes.

- **Other:** praise, clapping, jumping up and down, cheering, petting gently, petting roughly, just hanging out together, grabbing some grass or snow and tossing it up in the air.

Alert!
It's too easy to get stuck on using food as your only reinforcement type. Variable schedules and variable types of reinforcement require you to use creativity, imagination and forethought.

These are just a taste of the reinforcements you can use to reward your dog. Be creative and watch your dog to see what he likes.

You might think that applying life rewards, rather than giving the dog a piece of food, will slow down training. True, the session may take a bit longer, but in the long run, the behaviors trained will be learned faster, stay longer, and be stronger.

Pack Your Bags—We're Going to Hawaii!: Adding Surprise Elements

Being variable and unpredictable with forethought and planning is what makes someone a great trainer. While it may seem to be difficult at first, it becomes simple with practice. It becomes a way of life for many people because the benefits to the dog and to your mutual relationship are enormous and obvious.

What's more yummy? A plain banana, or a banana with three kinds of your favorite ice cream, plus hot fudge and chocolate sprinkles? Or how would you feel about packing for your vacation that you think will be to Colonial Williamsburg and your spouse surprises you with tickets to Hawaii?

Which do you think would be more fun for your dog? Eating the same old dry biscuit 10 times in a row for loose-leash walking, or getting one piece of tortellini, a scratch behind the ears, the chance to chase you, five pieces of hot dog, a short game of tug, and a belly rub for the same loose-leash walking?

The point is to be unpredictable, plan surprise rewards, be generous, be fun, be variable in how and when and how much you reinforce, and you'll have the trained dog of your dreams.

Using the methods in this book, you can become a great trainer. Great trainers ...

- Are good at reinforcing.

- Are quick and have good timing.

- Are unpredictable and vary when, how much, and how they apply reinforcers.

- Are variable and use many different types of reinforcers.

- Stop problems before they become locked in as solid behaviors.

- Plan their sessions carefully.

- Recognize small approximations and reward them.

- Keep a log or diary of each behavior being taught.

Pop Quiz

1. Which two schedules of reinforcement create a bored and noncompliant dog?

2. Which two schedules of reinforcement create a dog who will leap tall buildings in a single bound?

3. What is scalloping? (Hint: it isn't the fish.)

4. Have you started to use variable reinforcement while training? Are you seeing better results?

If you are seeing better results, give yourself a click and ice cream! If you aren't yet, you may want to plan your sessions before you bring your dog out—not only plan the behaviors you're working toward, but plan your reinforcers as well.

Summary

Fixed schedules of reinforcement kill behaviors.

Variable schedules of reinforcement create stronger behaviors and make training more fun and rewarding for your dog.

Plan surprise rewards for your dog.

Design a game strategy to become a great trainer.

Manipulation, Modern Style
The Premack Principle **13**

World renown psychologist David Premack developed the Premack Principle. It puts forth "the observation that high-probability behavior reinforces low-probability behavior." Essentially it means this: "Eat your vegetables and you can have dessert." To make this a bit easier to understand in terms of dog training, high-probability behaviors are what the dog wants; low-probability behaviors are what you want. In this chapter, you'll learn how to use this principle to get the behaviors you want from your dog.

Eat Your Vegetables First: What You Want

So what do you want from your dog? Think about this—really think. It's not easy, is it? Write it down if you have to. Come up with some concrete things you want from your dog. Otherwise, you don't know what you want from your dog! And if you don't know what you want, how are you supposed to train it? And how the heck is the dog supposed to know what you want? Dogs are very smart and may seem to be "almost human," but as of yet, I don't believe that dogs (or spouses or children) can actually read your mind.

Do you want your dog to sit quietly at the door when the leash is being put on? How about calm behaviors when walking down the street? Perhaps bringing the ball and dropping it at your feet rather than 20 feet away? Wouldn't you like to be able to peacefully sit and watch TV or prepare his food dish and put it on the floor without being pestered? Maybe you'd like him to stop straining at the leash to get to his doggie pal so that he can play. You can get all of these changes and more, by finding out what your dog wants and harnessing that desire.

> **Definitions**
> The Premack Principle states that high-probability behavior reinforces low-probability behavior.

After you've thought it over, write down your goals of exactly what you want from your dog. Now that you've written it down, it's time to figure out what your dog wants.

Hot Fudge Sundae: What Does Your Dog Want?

How will you know what your dog wants? Watch him carefully and write down what he enjoys most. Don't think you'll remember it all without writing it down, because you won't. Humor me and write it down anyway. It'll come in handy later.

Your dog might like to sniff; roll in smelly things; sniff; chase toys; play tug; play with other dogs; sniff; go swimming; go for a car ride; go for a walk, jog, or run; play in an open field; sniff; chase ducks, deer, or geese; herd sheep; find small rodents; be petted or massaged; sniff; practice agility; cuddle with you; sniff; get belly rubs; retrieve objects; sniff; eat food; pee on bushes (hopefully yours and not the neighbor's); get attention from you; be groomed (my dogs like to be groomed); and last but not least, sniff.

At this time you should have two lists—one with what you want and one with what your dog wants. Now let's put them together.

> ### Alert!
> Be sure to pick only those things that you would want to use as reinforcers later. Sock stealing, paper eating, garbage raiding, poop eating, furniture re-arranging or destructive chewing, and any type of behaviors you don't want,, shouldn't be on this list

The Art
Be creative and watch your dog. He'll tell you what he wants. It may change from day to day, hour to hour, and even minute to minute. That's okay—it gives you more reinforcers to choose from, hence "variety!"

The great thing about Premack is that your dog will very often learn to enjoy "lima beans"—what you want, be it a stay, loose-leash walking, being touched or groomed. So not only will he learn to accept a bunch of new things, but if you make what he wants contingent upon doing what you want, you will see an increase of tolerance and an increase of appropriate behaviors.

> ### Alert!
> If you "give in" to your dog for any of the behaviors he wants but you don't, then you're reinforcing the wrong behaviors. "Oh, but I drove all this way so that he could swim." Too bad, Bucko. If you're serious about wanting a change in certain behaviors, then don't give in to the unacceptable behaviors you don't want.

Becoming a Master Manipulator

You can make use of any of the things on your "what the dog wants" list to get what you want. Say you want to allow your dog to go swimming. You don't want him to drag you to the lake or pool. Make swimming dependent upon walking to the lake on a loose leash. No loose-leash walking, no swimming. If he doesn't walk nicely on the leash, just put him back in the car, wait for five to ten minutes, and try again. If, after three to four tries, he still hasn't noticed that you're alive, take him back home.

The Art
In the beginning, you may have to lower your criterion to start. A client has a dog that went insane when she saw water. The owner wanted to do loose leash walking to the lake; the dog wanted to go at top speed and drag her owner. So we started about

300 yards from the lake, got about three steps of heeling, and then raced with the dog to the lake and let her swim for a few minutes. The owner then said, "We'll never get her out of the water." Oh ye of little faith! Piece of cake! I encouraged her to come out of the water, gave her a treat and then instantly released her back in the water. By going back and forth — coming out of the water, doing some heeling and then a release back to the lake, within 30 minutes the dog was responding brilliantly and calmly — heeled when we asked, swam when we asked, and came out of the water when we asked.

Another client had two Beagles. Beagles have a natural tendency to have their noses on the ground 24/7. Why? Because we humans bred in that behavior. So instead of fighting their "Beagle-ness," we worked with it and exploited it. The first week, we asked (okay, we lured ... and then asked) for about one minute of attention and then let them go be Beagles for about 10 minutes. Then we repeated the process and asked for two minutes of attention, and then allowed 10 minutes of being a dog. By lesson number three, they were both glued to their owners for 15 to 20 minutes at a clip, and we did this outside in a 100 acre field!

The moral? Work with your dog, not against him, and you will have the dog of your dreams.

Your dog wants to go out, but you don't want him to jump up and down like an idiot when you try to put on his collar and leash. Ignore his jumping, and patiently wait. Once he's sitting calmly, put the leash on. If at any time he starts jumping again, stand still and wait. If it takes 15 minutes, then so be it. He will very quickly learn that if he sits quietly, he'll get to go for a walk faster. You can also work on the "collar" exercise in Chapter 7.

The key for Premacking anything is to know what your dog wants and then ask for what you want—be it calm behavior, eye contact, "Sit," "Down," "Stay," or whatever it is you want from him at the time.

Added Benefits

Let's say you have a dog who doesn't like to be touched. You can make touching a prerequisite to going outside. No touchy, no outside. Or no touchy, no bally. You don't have to start out with a full body rub. In fact, you shouldn't. Start with one light touch and then give the dog what he wants. Each day, you can add slightly more petting until you're eventually giving the dog a bear hug and before you know it, he's actually enjoying the handling.

The neat thing about Pre-macking is that the dog will very often learn to enjoy whatever behavior it is that you want — even if he doesn't like it at first. This is what "reinforcing low-probability behavior" means. The less likely of the two behaviors actually takes on more meaning for the dog. Now you have yet another way to reinforce your dog!

> ### *Details*
> Todd's dog Jesse hated to be handled in any way, but loved tennis balls. By lightly touching each and every body part before throwing the ball, over the course of a few months, Todd was able to groom and pet Jesse. In fact, Jesse learned to love petting so much that not only was Todd able to handle his dog, but their entire relationship changed for the better.

I've had many positive experiences with client dogs — some of which in the past, had to be sedated for simple procedures such as toe nail clipping and grooming. Just take your time, be clear and concise and you'll both get something you want!

Green Means Stop, Red Means Go: Giving Consistent Cues

Premack can backfire only if you're inconsistent. If sometimes you give in and sometimes you hold your ground, then guess what? Premack won't work for you. And your dog will still be pulling you on the leash, sniffing nonstop, or doing all the things that drive you insane. In fact, no dog training will work for you if you're inconsistent. Inconsistency is extremely frustrating for your dog, just as it is for humans.

How would you feel if today on the news they announced that tomorrow all green lights will mean stop and all red lights will mean go? We've been programmed to know the opposite, so even though we speak English, and understood the change in rules, we'd probably make many mistakes tomorrow. Accidents would happen and we'd get very angry.

Think about how your dog feels. He doesn't speak English. Really. You only think he does. So, if today "Come on" means come, and tomorrow "Let's go" means come, and the next day "Come" means loose-leash walking, and the day after that "Come here" means come ... well, you can see how frustrating your behavior can be to your dog and why your dog ignores you a lot of the time.

Pop Quiz

1. Come up with a list of 15 things your dog likes. (Don't forget, sock stealing, poop eating, and so on do not belong on this list.)

2. What is the definition of the Premack Principle?

3. How often do you (inadvertently) change your cues?

Summary

If you know what behavior you want from your dog, you can get that behavior by rewarding him with something you know he wants.

Before the dog gets what he wants, he must do what you want.
By using the Premack Principle in training, dogs often learn to enjoy the behavior that you want him to do.

When applying the Premack Principle, consistency is the secret to success.

What If My Dog Makes a Mistake 14

I'd like to share an experience I had at a seminar that may put it all into perspective for you. The question was, "What would have to happen in the environment for you to not go through a green light?" In other words, what would "trump" (override) the green light? Some answers included:

- The person in front of you didn't move (inhibition)

- Your car stalled (equipment failure)

- You hear a siren and can't tell where it's coming from (unsure)

- You see a car running a red light (unsafe)

- A loose horse ran across the road (yes, that actually happened to me!)

Proceeding through a green light is a cue drivers know very well and normally respond to quickly and without hesitation. So, in light of other factors, such as the ones above, are you being disobedient when you don't? No. In fact, you're doing just the right thing by intelligently not responding to that cue.

Why might a dog not respond to a truly known cue? What kinds of influences would make your dog be "disobedient?" For a dog, some possible answers could be:

- There's another strange dog or person close by that he can't safely take his eyes off of

- He isn't feeling well

- He has to pee, poop or is thirsty

- You've inadvertently changed your signal

- It's noisy and he didn't hear you

Like the drivers who didn't proceed through the green light, your dog isn't being disobedient — there are other factors in the environment that may cause him to not respond.

If a dog makes a mistake, you need to stop and look at the situation. Did you make the mistake—giving wrong or different cues or pushing the dog beyond his limits? Did you train the dog in enough contexts with enough correct repetitions? Were your expectations fair for the amount of training the dog has experienced?

Let's look at some different positive options to pursue when your dog makes a mistake. Not every tactic works for every dog or every situation, but there's always a positive solution if you take the time to look for it.

Proceed, Putting It on Cue

Two easy strategies for responding to an incorrect response are 1) proceed and 2) to put it on cue. These methods are great because they give you the chance to regroup, rethink, and go scream in the closet if you're getting angry. They also give you the opportunity to be creative in stopping some behaviors that are less than wonderful.

Proceed: Moving On to Something Else

After three tries, if your dog just isn't "getting it" today, instead of repeating the routine again and again (which can be seen as a punishment by the dog because he doesn't know how to change the outcome and has no opportunity for reinforcement), move on to something else or take a break.

Taking time for a breath, also gives you the opportunity to rethink your training strategy. It's very important to know exactly how to teach each behavior before you take the dog out for training. Most positive dog trainers have a plan for each training session, knowing what and how they're going to teach their dog. This plan entails:

- What behavior they will work on

- What approximation of that behavior they will accept

- How many repetitions they will do

- What they will do if the animal doesn't respond correctly

- What the reinforcers will be

- How many minutes each session will last

- How many minutes of downtime there will be between each session

- How many total sessions they will have per day

Putting It on Cue

While not my favorite option, although I have used it on occasion if the behavior isn't too "bad." It simply means to cue and reinforce the "bad" behavior you don't like so that the dog learns to perform the "bad" behavior only on cue. Then don't ever give the cue.

I did this with Beau, one of my Border Collies. On rainy days I have towels by the back door to wipe the dogs' feet as they come in from the backyard mud field. Well, Beau thought it was really cool to steal the towels and shred them.

So I put the "towel stealing" behavior on cue. I called it "mop the floor" (because he likes to shake the towel, pretending that he's killing it). In the beginning, I would say, "Mop the floor" for stealing a towel and then click and treat him. I did this dozens of times, and now on rainy days he will not take a towel unless I say, "Mop the floor."

As they say, "If you can't beat 'em, join 'em." Or in the dog-training world we say, "Put it under stimulus control and never give the cue!"

> ### Definition
> Stimulus control means that the dog responds promptly to a cue in any and all situations. Some people say that barking can be put under stimulus control, but I've never seen it work. Barking seems to be an incredibly self-reinforcing behavior for many dogs, and they'll do it anyway, cued or not.

Management, Aid, Antecedent

The key is to set the dog up to be right. It's counterproductive, not to mention silly, to set the dog up to fail and then get angry at him for failing. Being frustrated is normal, and taking it out on the dog is easy. Your dog doesn't speak English and sometimes that makes training hard. However, there are easy answers.

If your dog eats your shoes, put them away! If your dog gets into the garbage can, find one with a locking lid. If you know a certain stimulus upsets or overexcites your dog, use better judgment in introducing the stimulus to your dog. Then work on desensitizing your dog to it.

The Art

Don't wait for something "bad" to happen—stop the behavior before it starts. Be pro-active, not reactive. Being pro-active — not letting the bad behavior happen in the first place, is the best course with the highest payback. Being reactive will teach him nothing because the inappropriate behavior has already happened. Practicing "bad" behaviors does no one any good. Plus, it might make you angry and you may do something that you'll regret in the morning. After all, you would baby-proof a house, and you should doggie-proof it as well.

Aid

Give the dog an easier version of the behavior you're working on that he can solve successfully: shorten the time, distance, duration, or complexity.

For instance, let's say you're teaching your dog to "Stay," and you've built up to one minute in an area that has no distractions. Good job! Now you go to the ballgame, which is much more diverting than your empty living room. Don't ask your dog to "Stay" for one minute—he won't be successful. Try for three seconds to start, and build slowly back up to one minute.

Antecedent

Give the dog some clear, intermediate helper cues so that he can understand more clearly what it is you want. This can be a verbal reminder cue, "Stay," or an additional hand signal. The key is not to do rapid-fire reminder cues—then you get stuck in the rut of "Sit-Sit-Sit-Sit-Sit" and sound like a machine gun. Dogs don't speak English, but they sure can count! Don't confuse them even more when your task is to help them.

In addition, be sure that your cues are consistent and accurate. If sometimes you call your dog to "Come" and you're standing up straight, and sometimes bending over, or sitting, or kneeling, you'll have one very confused doggie. If your cue for "Down" is normally a raised hand like a traffic cop but one day you just raise your hand high in the sky, don't be surprised when the dog looks at you blankly.

Incompatible, Ignore, Innovation

Now is the time to get a bit inventive. I've given you some of my favorite options to jump-start your creative juices. Incompatible behaviors will save your sanity, so teach your dog to do all of the behaviors in this book—they are all "incompatible" with fear, aggression, and nervousness. They also give the dog a "job" to do. If you don't give your dog a job, he will become self-employed, and you most likely won't like the career change.

Give your dog a cue (one that he knows well) that's incompatible with the "bad" behavior he's doing at the moment. For instance, if you tell the dog to "Sit," that's an incompatible behavior to jumping. He can't be jumping if he's sitting. Or, once your dog has excellent name recognition (see Chapter 5), you can say his name to get his attention and then give him a cue to a different behavior to keep him otherwise occupied.

Training incompatible behaviors is one of my favorite ways of solving behavior problems. Sometimes it just takes a bit of thought to come up with a solution. If your dog goes crazy every time the doorbell rings, train him that the sound of the doorbell means "Go to your crate." Let's say that every time your dog sees someone, he wants to fling himself at that person. Teach him that a person approaching is a cue to sit. Or if you want to allow him to approach a person, teach him to "Go visit," meaning to go to the person you're pointing to and lie down—which is incompatible to jumping.

Ignoring the Dog

If the dog is doing something bad, ignore him until he gives you a "good" behavior that you can then reinforce. For example, if your dog is barking at someone or something, just stand still until he's quiet, wait for 10 seconds, and then reinforce the quiet behavior. By yelling or petting to calm him down, you're actually reinforcing the inappropriate behavior. If, after 15 seconds or so, the dog hasn't regained control of himself, move away, redirect onto appropriate behaviors, and then reinforce the dog for "good" behaviors.

If the dog is ignoring you, leave the area and have him search for you. Let him know that you aren't irrelevant or just a piece of furniture that happens to be at the end of the leash. Please use good judgment when walking away from your dog during training. Don't disappear if the area isn't safe and secure to leave your dog.

Details

Here's a quiz: Kate had problems with her 14-month-old dog, Chloë. Chloë was constantly jumping and biting for attention, which she'd been doing this since she was 12 weeks old. If she didn't get instant attention, Chloë would become more frantic and bite harder, especially if there was food around.

Question: Why was Chloë doing this, and what can be done to stop it?

Answer: Kate admitted to reinforcing the jumping and mouthing by giving Chloë attention by petting or yelling at her. To fix Chloë's behavior, Kate should ignore her inappropriate behaviors and reward her heavily for not bothering humans and for being calm around food; she could also teach Chloë to do really a fast "Sit" (since sitting is incompatible with jumping and biting).

Innovation

Try changing your rewards to something new that the dog really craves. No matter how much you like M&M's, there's probably a level at which you will satiate, and the same thing happens to your dog. Use all different types of food, toys, silly games, petting, and praise to reinforce your dog.

Being variable and unpredictable is the key to enriching your dog's life and keeping training fun. Chapter 12 has a full discussion on the "how" of variable reinforcement.

Repeat, Redirect, Recreation, Restrain

Watch and listen to your dog. If you pay attention to what he is telling you, most of the time you can come up with an easy solution. If you have a good relationship with your dog, he really does want to do what you're asking of him. If all of a sudden he looks at you blankly, please don't assume that he's stupid.

Try one more time by using clearer cues, such as a hand signal. Wait for at least 10 seconds before repeating the cue so that the dog learns to perform immediately after the first cue. Don't repeat it a third time! You don't want your cue to be "Sitsitsit!"

By waiting patiently for at least 10 seconds, you're giving the dog the opportunity to think! Remember when you were first learning a foreign language? Did you remember all of those new words the first time out? In addition, don't forget: humans are a verbal species and dogs are not!

Redirect

Redirect to better behavior. If your dog eats the sofa, learn what he usually does just before eating the sofa—sniffing the floor, running around, barking, or whining—and stop the sofa destruction before it happens. Be proactive, not reactive! You can distract him with a toy when he just starts to think about eating the sofa (or preferably before he even thinks about it), but be sure that you don't then try to play with him after he has already started. This will only reinforce the sofa-eating behavior. You can still distract, but then give him at least three other behaviors to do and then reinforce him.

Dogs who incessantly bark or chew are usually under-stimulated or bored or have been inadvertently reinforced (with your attention or bad timing of reinforcement) for doing the very behavior that's driving you crazy. Remember: behavior is reward driven!

Be sure to pay plenty of attention to your dog when he's not doing anything "bad"!

Recreation

Use tiredness to your advantage: a dog who is fully exercised, both mentally and physically, is less likely to bark, chew, jump up, or otherwise drive you insane. Giving the dog enough vigorous exercise with you is excellent preventive therapy! My motto is, "A tired dog is a good dog." A placid walk around the block is not enough aerobic exercise to physically tire out most dogs. Playing fetch, swimming, playing with another dog, jogging, mental puzzles and hiking are all good ways to keep your dog fit and to tire him out. This is the ultimate incompatible behavior: a sleeping dog can do no harm.

> *Details*
> I prefer activities that the two of you can do together. Because classical conditioning (remember Ivan Pavlov?) is always happening, you might as well take advantage of it and pair yourself with all sorts of fun things for your dog. That way, you have a tired dog and a dog that associates good stuff with you. It's a win-win situation.

Restrain

Confine or contain the dog. But be sensible! If imminent danger threatens, get your dog out of there! If the dog is veering off into traffic, or a loose dog in attack mode is coming at you and your dog, get out of there! Although it's preferable to wait out a "bad" reaction from your dog so that you can then reinforce "good" behavior, there are times when a fast retreat is best. If the dog is so incredibly over-aroused that he's foaming at the mouth, spit is flying everywhere, and his eyes are glazed, then the window of opportunity has closed! Get him out of there—now!

There's time enough later, when everyone is calm, to assess the situation dispassionately and carefully. If the situation was something out of your control— such as a loose dog with no owner in sight—you can read Chapter 3, on familiarizing yourself with calming signals. Many times you can use these to "disarm" a dog who is showing aggressive behaviors.

> *Details*
> Patty was out with her dog Mike when they came upon a loose dog running around, growling at every dog in his path. There was no way of restraining the loose dog, so Patty quickly and calmly asked Mike to lie down (a calming signal). She kept Mike's attention on her, rather than risk his reacting to the errant dog. The instant Mike lay down, the approaching dog slowed his pace, sniffed Mike in a halfhearted fashion, and then went about his doggie way.

Above all, think about what you're doing to encourage your dog to behave in a certain way. If your dog does something you don't like on a regular basis, watch yourself to see whether you're inadvertently reinforcing the dog for doing that very behavior!

For instance, if your dog repeatedly steals your clothes and then you chase after him in a merry game of keep-away, your dog thinks "What fun, Mommy! Thanks!" Do you yell at the dog? (Remember—negative attention is still attention.) Now he thinks, "Wow, Mom is turning purple and chasing me all over the house! Thanks, Mom!" Before getting angry, think to yourself, "What is the dog finding reinforcing in this situation?

So, before judging the dog poorly, look back and rethink!

Pop Quiz

1. Have you started planning your sessions better?

2. Name at least five alternative options you can utilize if your dog makes a mistake.

3. Have you inadvertently reinforced your dog for any "bad" behaviors?

Summary

If your dog doesn't respond correctly after three tries, move on to something else.

Stop "bad" behaviors before they start; help by setting your dog up for success.

If your dog does something you don't like, redirect him to an incompatible behavior, such as lying down.

Be proactive, not reactive!

Positive Solutions to "Bad" Behavior 15

"If you always do what you've always done, then you'll always get what you've always got." Henry Ford.

I gotta tell you, I personally trained my own dogs to commit all sorts of obnoxious behaviors before I knew better. I trained my Sheltie, Noel, to bark for four hours while I prepared her dinner. I taught my other Sheltie, Cody, to hate his dumbbell, and I allowed Cody to teach Beau and Shadow to fence chase (to run along the fence line while barking).

Will I ever stop teaching my dogs "bad" behaviors? Probably not, because to err is human, and to forgive, canine. But I never blame the dogs, because I know that I'm the one who trained them to commit their "bad" behaviors. I stop it as soon as I see something happening that I didn't want and never let it get too far into "badness."

One of the hardest things for humans to comprehend is that dogs are really smart and quickly learn exactly what we teach them. The problem is that we humans teach them the wrong behaviors! We don't do this on purpose of course, but we do it nonetheless.

Day after day, week after week, year after year, I see people repeatedly reinforcing what they don't want! Then they get angry at the dog, perhaps thinking that they have a stupid or stubborn dog. In reality, the dog is actually quite clever and is doing exactly what he was trained to do.

One Dog's Punishment Is Another's Reinforcement

It's not up to you to decide what's reinforcing (or punishing) to your dog—it's your dog's choice. One of my own dogs—Beau—hates tortellini and acts like I am trying to poison him, yet Cody would kill for tortellini. I've seen some dogs who love to be sprayed in the face with water and other dogs who find this very punishing.

If it suppresses behavior, it's a punishment. If it increases behavior, it's a reinforcer. Don't forget, though, that while punishment does in fact suppress behavior; it doesn't eliminate it. It may stop the behavior for a short time, but the behavior always comes back at one time or another. SUPPRESSION ISN'T CURE, and can have toxic side effects. The following sections discuss some of the behaviors that are probably on your list and what you can do about them.

Barking

Your dog barks incessantly and you ignore him up to a point. Then you start barking (yelling) along with the dog, thus reinforcing the dog's barking. Barking is a very hard behavior to stop because there are so many triggers for it. Real or imagined noises, sights, smells, other animals, kids, and fast movements are just a few of the eight zillion prompts for barking. If your lifestyle won't support a dog that barks, do your research first into your breed of choice to make sure you don't pick a breed that was bred to bark!

Some dogs learn to use barking to get your attention. Many dogs bark because (it seems, anyway) they like to hear themselves talk. Shetland Sheepdogs bark at the footfall of a squirrel from two days ago. Some dogs bark out of stress, arousal, or even boredom (which can also be stressful). And some breeds, such as Beagles, Akbash, Great Pyrenees, Anatolian Shepherd Dogs, Nova Scotia Duck Tolling Retrievers, Shetland Sheepdogs, American Eskimos and Lhasa Apsos, were specifically bred to bark as part of their jobs (such as herding, hunting, and guarding).

As hard as this may seem, the best thing to do is to completely ignore the dog. Walk out of the room, put earplugs in, do whatever you have to do to not react to your dog. Then after five seconds to five minutes of no barking (depending on the length of time the dog was barking), reinforce the dog for the quiet behavior. The longer the dog barks, the longer the quiet behavior should be. Reinforce too soon after five minutes of barking and that will be what you'll get more of.

If you give in and respond to the dog's barking after, let's say, three minutes, then you've just reinforced three minutes of barking. If you then try again and blow your cool after 10 minutes, you've now reinforced 10 minutes of barking. You get the picture. That's how I taught Noel to bark for four hours. Please learn from my mistake.

> ### *Alert!*
> Just as we speak, dogs bark. Reducing or even eliminating barking from the dog's behavior repertoire is not impossible, it just isn't the easiest "bad" behavior to change, especially if you've been reinforcing it in the past.

No matter the situation, if you know your dog will react, manage the environment so as to set him up to be quiet. If he barks in crowds, stay farther away and reinforce quiet behaviors. If he barks at kids running, enlist the neighborhood kids to help you. Have them walk by slowly, reinforcing your dog for not barking. Then have them slowly jog by, then run by, and then maybe even add that ear-piercing scream that most kids know how to do, all the while reinforcing your dog for quiet behaviors.

Almost Sure-Fire Way to Minimize Barking: "Uncle Fred"

You're going to think I've gone off the deep end with my "Uncle Fred" solution, but really, it works 99% of the time. If your dog is barking at your door or front window, walk up to him, look out, right and left and no matter what is or isn't there, say in a nonchalant voice, "Oh, it's only Uncle Fred" and walk away. Nine times out of ten, your dog will come with you when you leave, so reinforce him for doing so. For some bizarre reason, this only works with "Uncle Fred."

My theory is this (which I have to admit, I totally made up and have no real notion if it is correct — but it works): underling wolves let the wolf in charge know if there is an intruder. Then, the leader wolf decides what to do — ignore or repel with force. Now, we aren't wolves and neither are our dogs, however, if you let your dog know, "Don't worry, I'll handle it," they usually just stop barking.

Alert Barking

Let's say you do in fact want your dog to bark to alert you if someone is coming (not really a bad thing — barking dogs usually repel people that are thinking about breaking and entering).

Have someone outside that will knock on your cue (use your cell phone to communicate when they should start and stop knocking). They knock, your dog barks, you interrupt after the third bark by clicking and then treat. This is an exercise in timing for you because you only want to allow him three barks. It takes an average of 40 minutes for the dog to figure out that three barks are allowed and to come and find you after the third one.

Jumping

Say your dog jumps on people who come to the door. Dogs jump to greet people— it is a natural submissive greeting behavior and they have to jump because we're taller than they are. Oddly enough (from a human standpoint), the dog thinks that by offering these submissive behaviors, he's being very polite.

Half of the people will pet the dog, reinforcing the dog for jumping. You've heard them say: "Oh, it's okay; I love dogs." The other half will yank the dog down, squeeze his paws until he is screaming in pain, or knee him in the chest. Or you may yank the dog down or yell at him in your embarrassment of his behavior.

> *Pointers*
> Contrary to old-fashioned beliefs, jumping up is not a sign of dominance or aggression.

All of these reactions reinforce the dog for jumping—including the negative reactions. Punish the dog for jumping and he may feel the need to jump even more in a more submissive, frantic manner to appease your anger, increasing the cycle of jumping on people. Or the dog may decide that people are dangerous (since so much punishment happens around people) and, as you have learned in previous chapters, the jumping may intensify into fearful biting behaviors or extreme shyness.

Solutions for jumping

These are some of my favorite options that you can adopt to teach your dog that "four on the floor" is more rewarding than jumping:

- Avert your eyes and turn sideways as he's about to jump—you can always see the signs in their little eyes or in their bodies! If you miss the signals and the dog jumps, still turn sideways to deflect the dog. Then once he has four on the floor, wait passively for five seconds, ask him to "Sit," and then reinforce.

- You can also walk away slowly (a calming signal) and reinforce the dog for staying on the ground. Throw treats on the floor to further reinforce that "down there" is better. Play the "rev up and cool down" game in Chapter 11.

- Become a tree stump. Don't move. After all, how reinforcing can a tree stump be? Have you ever seen a dog jump repeatedly on a tree stump? Don't look at the dog and don't talk to the dog or push him away. Trees don't have eyes, ears, mouths, or arms. Just stand there. He'll eventually get down. Wait for five seconds, ask him to "Sit," and then reinforce.

- Teach the dog to jump on cue by encouraging him to jump and saying "Up" when he does. Give him a quick pet and murmur "Good." Then look away and become a stump. When you feel the dog get off, say "Off" and have a party! Give him the jackpot of his life—tons of food, calm petting, praise, and lots of attention. Repeat a billion times. He'll soon learn that the reward for not jumping is infinitely better than the reward for jumping.

- One of my favorite options is to teach the dog to "Go visit." "Go visit" means that on your cue only, the dog goes up to the person you're pointing to and lies down! (Lying down is incompatible with jumping.)

Go Visit (a.k.a. The Two Trainer Game)

You'll need two people for this, both armed with treats.

1. You point to your helper and say "go visit." Then you say nothing.

2. Helper calls the dog.

3. Helper then asks your dog to sit and down and heavily reinforces the down.

4. Helper then says, "Go see Mommy (or Daddy)"

5. You call your dog back to you and reinforce the recall

Repeat this about eight to ten times and your helper will start to fade out any cues to sit or down — just wait for a few seconds to see if the dog has picked up the pattern. When he does down on his own — jackpot!

I love this exercise not only for not jumping, but because it gets your dog to come away from a big distraction — someone with food.

Person Approaching = Sit

You'll need a helper for this game as well. Have your dog contained behind a barrier or on a leash (preferably on a harness). You stand still — your only job is to just stand still and don't yank back.

1. Helper (has treats) and approaches your dog and asks for a sit before the dog jumps

2. Reward dog if he sits

3. If he starts to jump, helper turns around and leaves

4. Helper returns and asks for a sit again and rewards

5. Helper repeats steps 1 and 2. Usually within three to four reps, the dog will automatically sit

If your dog jumps wildly on people coming to the door, make the doorbell a cue to go to his crate.

> ***Alert!***
> Be sure to only use people who will take instruction from you and not do what they see on T.V. We don't want people kicking your dog or giving what they think are the correct cues.

Excuse Me

If your dog still doesn't react appropriately to the above options, try the "excuse me" cue.

1. Ask your dog to stand.

2. Step into him perpendicularly, but be sure not to touch him. Just lean into him and he should yield (i.e. Move away from your pressure).

3. Click and throw the treat on the floor and repeat six to ten times.

4. Once he is yielding, you can name it "excuse me" as he is moving away.

5. Don't step directly into his front — otherwise he'll just sit and won't be able to get out of your way.

6. You can start to say "excuse me" the instant you see he is about to jump up. If need be, you can just take one step toward him and he'll check himself.

Excuse me is also a wonderful cue to use when you're racing to the phone and he gets in your way.

Details
Mark came in with his five-month-old Boxer, Merlin, and his four-and-a-half-year-old daughter Jean. Merlin was body-slamming Jean to the ground on a daily basis. Within one hour, Merlin stopped knocking Jean over, and it has lasted ten years so far. Was it magic?

Nope—I just taught Jean to use head turns, body turns, and walking away slowly to reinforce Merlin for being on the ground. The relationship between the two has improved so much so that now Jean is the main trainer of the dog! If a four-and-a-half-year-old child can do it, so can you!

Nipping and mouthing
"Ouch! There he goes again! Stop it. Stop it. I said stop it! This dog is driving me crazy!" Sound familiar? Biting, like jumping, can be inadvertently reinforced by your actions. In fact, the cures for biting are similar to those for jumping.

Pointers
When was the last time your dog got together with Muffy from down the street to play Parcheesi? Not in your recent memory? Maybe they do when all the humans are sleeping? I think not. Dogs play by biting, body slamming, chasing, humping, growling, barking, and knocking over furniture. This is normal dog play behavior. It's not aggression—even if it's directed at you.

Dogs bite for many reasons: because they can, because that's how they play with other dogs, because they get a "rise" out of us, and because it's fun.

If your dog bites you or mouths you, use the calming signals you learned in Chapter 3—turn sideways, yawn, move slowly away, or sit or lie down (if possible, without being further mauled).

Watch for any patterns of when the biting or mouthing behaviors start. Is it a certain time of day, are you ignoring the dog, or are you overexciting the dog with too-rough play? Is the dog under-exercised, overfed, or bored?

If he bites you at a certain time of day or when you are too busy to pay attention to him, you have two options: you can start engaging him in play before he starts, or you can completely walk away and ignore him. Put a barrier between the two of you if necessary or go into another room and shut the door. You must be silent, however, and you can't be silent when you're in pain, so this should be a good incentive for you to watch your dog and stop the biting behavior before it starts!

If your dog is under-exercised and overfed, well, you know what you have to do. Get up off the couch and go outside! Walking sedately around the block on a six-foot leash is not enough aerobic exercise for a normal dog. He needs running, swimming, chasing toys, hiking, long walks in the woods, and whatever else you can think of that your dog likes.

> **Pointers**
> If your dog bites when you're trying to handle or groom him, review the handling guide in Chapter 7.

When I deal with puppies, the instant I feel teeth, I go limp and give a few calming signals — a yawn, a blink, a head turn or a lip lick. Usually within a few seconds, the pup disengages and goes tottering off.

> **Pointers**
> I boarded a puppy for two weeks. This puppy was really nipping his owners constantly - all day long. I tried to see if I could get the pup to nip me so I could then fix it for them. Obviously I didn't go out of my way to be horrible to the dog, but I pet him all over and manipulated him and not once in two weeks did he ever touch me with his mouth. The instant the owners came to pick him up, he went wild nipping them.
>
> Why would this be? Because I didn't have a history of reinforcing him for nipping me and the owners did.

You may be stressing out your dog more than you think by playing too rough with him. You get rougher and he doesn't know how to get you to stop, so he bites you. Should you be angry? Not! You're the one who pushed him too far. If this is happening to you, you have some choices. Stop roughhousing with the dog using your hands and body and use toys instead. Or if you insist on playing with him with your not-puncture-resistant arms and hands, stop the play before your dog gets too aroused or stressed. Then pet him lightly and gently to calm him down completely.

Biting the Kids

The issue of children and dogs together can run the gamut from annoying yet benign to a serious, dangerous one. Because of the potential seriousness of the issue, I am not going to address it in this book. If your dog is biting your children or you're feeling uncomfortable, then find a qualified trainer to help you. See Appendix.

Can Dogs Really Have Selective Deafness?

Does your dog ignore you when you want to train? Does he periodically have "selective deafness?" You cheerlead and possibly bribe with a treat to try to get the dog's attention. When he finally does come to you, you may play with him or give him a treat. He now ignores you more and more for longer and longer periods of time. What were you really reinforcing? The inattention!

Details

Fran came in with her Golden Retriever, Dexter, for lessons. Dexter had a really bad case of selective deafness and would ignore Fran about 99% of the time. I put them on a "work for a living" program and the results were astounding. Fran was so pleased with Dexter's new-found focus in just one week that she continued to feed Dexter all of his meals from her hand for "jobs."

Go back to the basics from Chapter 5: eye contact, name, recall word, and praise word recognition.

Hand-feed the dog for two weeks—not for free, but for specific behaviors such as "Sit," "Down," eye contact, or anything the dog knows how to do. You can "insist" on eye contact going through doors, in and out of the car, in and out of the crate, and from one location to another. Follow these steps:

1. Wait for 30 seconds for the dog to give you eye contact. If he doesn't give you eye contact (with no verbal prodding from you), he gets a trip back to the crate (with no emotion from you; you should periodically give the dog a treat for going back in the crate—yes, even for "failing").

2. Repeat again and again until you get eye contact within 30 seconds.

3. Next, raise your criteria and now wait for only 25 seconds before sending the dog back to his crate. Repeat again and again until you get eye contact within 25 seconds.

4. Then raise your criteria and lower the amount of time that you wait for eye contact.

5. Keep repeating until you get eye contact within three seconds. Once your dog is looking at you within three seconds, you can start working on whatever behaviors you want. If you lose the dog's attention, wait three seconds to see whether you can get it back (again, no verbal prompting from you). If not, back to the crate he goes.

Most people find that this process takes a few weeks or months—depending on how long they've reinforced the dog's inattention. Don't lower your criteria just because you want to train for a specific amount of time or have some other goal in mind. If you do, you'll shoot yourself in the foot by starting the cycle of inattention again. Attention is the foundation of all training and should never be taken for granted.

Pop Quiz

1. In the past, have you inadvertently reinforced your dog for barking, jumping, and so on?

2. If your dog is biting you, look to yourself—are you stressing him? Is he overfed and underworked? Is anyone in the family playing too rough with him?

Summary

Every time you yell at your dog, hit him, or punish him in any way for barking, jumping, or biting, you're reinforcing those behaviors.

If you make an "issue" of jumping and biting, they will become rock-solid behaviors.

Concentrate on teaching your dog alternate behaviors and watch him carefully for signs that you are pushing him too hard.

If you aren't ignoring a bad behavior, then you're reinforcing it.

Use calming signals — Go limp

Walk away

Be silent

Nala problems —

Pushing

Mouthing

Barking

Doorways — won't go in at al
ie whatever I want

Barking at 'strange' people
usually men.

Side Effects of Punishment 16

Dogs are not humans. Sounds pretty obvious, doesn't it? Maybe you're thinking, "Why are you telling me this? Of course I know my dog is not human!" Well, you may "know" it, but because we are humans, we do "human" things and handle our dogs in a "human" way. We can't help it. Therein lies the problem. How many of us treat inanimate objects as human? We yell at the toaster, TV, and of course, let's not forget our cars when they don't start! Getting angry at these objects obviously doesn't make them work any better. Getting angry or punishing your dog will not only not make him better behaved, but can also create some serious side effects.

Punishment can create so many toxic side effects, I'd be afraid to use it. That doesn't mean that sometimes I'm not tempted—I'm human after all, and at times my dogs annoy the heck out of me. But I never resort to it. Increased use of punishment does not stop "bad" behaviors. They just get worse.

Some dogs may tolerate more punishment than others. Some of them are happy, willing workers—or seem to be. After a while, however, they may shut down and refuse to work, or may develop neurotic behaviors that seemingly came out of nowhere.

What Is Punishment?

So what constitutes punishment to a dog? The sky's the limit here—verbal reprimands, yelling, screaming, hitting, spanking, slapping, leash jerks, shock collars, head halters, choke collars, hoses, spray bottles, soda cans with pennies in them, citronella collars—anything that's meant to stop behaviors in a negative way.

A mommy dog may grab a puppy dog by the neck and reprimand the pup. What we as humans fail to see are the "okay, okay, I'll stop" signs that the puppy gives. Mommy dog does see these signs and releases immediately. Humans are simply incapable of detecting those signs because we are not dogs.

If you try to do this to a dog and the dog says "uncle," you have no clue and continue on. What can this cause? The pup will now get really upset and confused because he has been trying to say he is "sorry," and yet you continue to pound him. He may then bite, growl, or become afraid of you. Perhaps the behavior you were trying to "correct" didn't warrant such a harsh punishment and he may feel the need to protect himself.

Now you have trained your dog that even if he submits, he is going to be punished anyway. This will often lead to an aggressive, fearful dog or one that goes into learned helplessness because he is not able to get the punishment to stop.

Escalating Punishment

Say your dog pulls on the leash. The first time, you yank him back. The next time, you yell at him. The third time, you hit him. Now you put a prong collar on him and continue to hit, yell, scream, and yank back. He is still pulling on the leash. And now, because of the punishment and bad associations, he's possibly aggressing at people or dogs, and congratulations! You have now created a leash-aggressive dog!

> **Definition**
> Learned Helplessness occurs when the dog (or human) just shuts down because nothing he does is ever right.

Your dog jumps on people coming to the door. Today you push him down. He comes back for more. You push him down harder. Up he goes again. You knee him in the chest. He finally stops jumping. You are positively reinforced for using punishment because "it worked!"

Tomorrow he is jumping again. You start with kneeing him in the chest—because "it worked yesterday." It isn't working today, so you squeeze his paws so tightly that he screams in pain. He stops jumping—today. You are reinforced again for using punishment: "Okay, now I get it—I have to squeeze his paws until he screams." And what will you do tomorrow?

Observable Effects of Punishment

We can't assume (because we all know what happens when we assume) that we know how an animal is feeling or what he's thinking, but we can observe and measure behaviors. Be careful when observing, though—some of these behaviors, especially avoidance, look to us imperfect humans as "guilt." They are not. Punish your dog and any of these six behaviors may happen, which can be reliably observed and measured:

- Anxiety: Measurable by body chemistry

- Fear: Observable behavior

- Escape: Observable behavior

- Avoidance: Observable behavior

- Aggression: Observable behavior

- Learned helplessness: Observable behavior

Many people will then punish their dog for displaying these behaviors, which only escalates the dog's response.

Causes of "Bad" Behaviors

There are many causes of "bad" behaviors, most of which we can alleviate. The top three sources are the following:

- Punishment from humans

- Punishment from other animals

- Punishment from the environment

Additional stimuli that can create different levels of arousal include thunder, grooming, vet visits, invasive people, other dogs, other animals, cars, bikes, kids, being left alone, large groups, buildings, petting, toenail clipping, being on leash, men, hats, umbrellas, grass, concrete, gravel, linoleum, balloons … you name it, there's a dog out there afraid of it.

What is the root of these problems? It can be many things including improper socialization, or no socialization at all. An owner may mistakenly manage the dog's environment too much and to such a degree that the dog is never, in the critical early stages, exposed to loud noises, pots dropping, new sights, and so on. Once the dog gets older and these daily things occur, the dog freaks out. You certainly don't want to overexpose your young dog, but in real life, "stuff happens." A fearful mother dog can pass along her neurosis. But a biggie in the equation is punishment from us, for reacting out of nervousness or fear.

You may do one of two things when your dog shows signs of fear:

- Try to soothe and pet the dog: "It's okay Rover, Uncle Bob won't bite you."

- Yell and smack the dog: "Don't you dare growl at Aunt Helen!"

Either way you respond is reinforcing the dog for the behavior you don't want. If you try to comfort the dog, the dog may be reinforced for the fearful or aggressive behaviors. I don't mean this as a blanket statement, as in never re-assure your dog, but just take note of the unwanted behavior increasing or decreasing and act accordingly. For instance, I had a dog that was terrified of thunder. When I cuddled her, her fear increased. When I ignored her, she presented less fear and just laid down next to me because I didn't make a big deal of it.

If you punish the dog, still thinking that you have to "show" the dog when he's wrong (although how a dog can be "wrong" for being afraid is beyond me), you're creating the wrong association—he then learns that bad things happen around that stimulus (be it a person or dog or whatever). Since the dog is already in stress mode, where he's unable to think at all, you have just added even more stress and pain. The next time he encounters that particular stimulus, his negative reaction will intensify and escalate faster.

More often than not, it's our reactions or punishment that create worse problems than what we started with. What may have started out as mild anxiety can quickly grow into full-blown fear and avoidance.

Pointers
What we humans may view as benign may be perceived by an individual dog as being horrible. It's not up to us to decide for our dogs, or anyone else for that matter, what's scary or not scary. I love thunderstorms, yet one of my friends is so afraid of them, she hides in the

---

Anxiety and Fear

What's happening after you punish the dog either verbally or physically? He may become anxious and try to appease and diffuse your anger with submissive doggie gestures. Some of the signs of a dog's anxiety that we humans incorrectly perceive as "looking guilty" may be a lowered head, tail tucked between legs, ears back, and even a submissive grin. We assume (there's that word again) that the dog "knows what he did wrong."

The observable signs of anxiety can also include the following:

- Nervousness
- Whining
- Sniffing
- Barking
- Pacing
- Drooling
- Yawning
- Chewing
- Obsessive licking (licking feet or body parts compulsively to cause sores — also called lick granuloma)
- Inattention to owner and many of the signals listed in Chapter 3

Detail
A woman called me to ask about housetraining. Her dog runs away from her when she tries to approach. When I asked her what she was doing, she said she was hitting the dog for soiling the house. I explained that punishment is not the proper or effective way to housetrain a dog. Her response was, "Oh, I don't punish my dog, I only hit her."

Think about it from your own perspective: you have a boss who's very punishing— nothing you ever do is right. You go to work each day with a heavy heart and dragging feet. You start to develop physical or emotional symptoms related to anxiety. You may still be able to function, but you'll be sure to do the absolute minimum required, cut corners, and shirk responsibility wherever possible.

> ### *Detail*
> Before I found a wonderful computer technician, if I was having problems with a program, I would yell, scream, rant, and rave, and all but smash my computer with a sledge hammer. My dogs would then freak out at my behavior and display all sorts of appeasement behaviors at me (such as jumping, pawing at me, licking, frantic tail wagging, hiding under the table, etc.), thinking I was screaming at them. This, of course, would make me even angrier, so I learned that if I was about to beat my computer to death, I would put the dogs out in the

To think that our dogs will suffer no side effects when we punish them is just downright unreasonable. Of course there are side effects! If there were no effects of punishment, then "anxiety" wouldn't be in the dictionary!

Fear is another consequence of using punishment. Some of the signs of fear can be the following:

- Hiding
- Wide eyes
- Backing away
- Shaking
- Hackles up
- Growling
- Evacuation of bowels

You're out walking your dog and it starts raining. Your dog sees an umbrella for the first time and is terrified. He starts to shake, his hackles go up, and he tries vehemently to get away from this horribly scary thing. You're embarrassed by his behavior in such a public place and you chastise him. The next time you innocently pop open the umbrella, he may very well start to growl, shake, or evacuate his bowels. I'm sure you've observed these types of behaviors at the vet's office.

Maybe you're from the school of thought that advocates, "Don't punish unless you catch him in the act." If so, you then lay in wait for him to soil in the house and then whammo! You punish the dog. What has the dog learned? To be afraid of you, to run and hide, and to soil behind the couch where you can't see him because eliminating around you is dangerous. Now when you take your dog out for a "potty" walk, he won't do his business while on leash because you're standing right there. Another version is that your dog soils the house in your absence. You come home and yell at him. Of course, he has no clue why you're punishing him. So he learns that "homecoming" is a stressful and fearful time.

Escape and Avoidance

Next up on the countdown of behaviors caused by punishment are escape and avoidance. They're actually quite similar—it all depends on how the dog manifests them.

Escape can include the following:

- Running away
- Digging out of the yard or kennel
- Scratching at doors
- Hiding under or behind furniture
- Slipping out of collars

If your dog would rather be lost in the woods, eat bark from trees, sleep out in the raw elements without any of the creature comforts such as air-conditioning, heat, running water, three square meals per day, and a soft bed than be with you, then you may want to re-examine your relationship with your dog.

If, at the slightest opportunity, your dog flies out of the door ("I'm outta here!"), what do you think may be the problem? The correct answer should not have in it this statement: "My dog is a (fill in the breed here), so of course he runs away." Breed has nothing to do with a dog's running away—chances are you're using punishment to train your dog and he wants to get away from it.

Avoidance is the second half of this equation. There are two kinds of avoidance: passive avoidance and active avoidance. Passive avoidance includes the following:

- Ignoring
- Avoiding eye contact or petting
- "Selective deafness"

Active avoidance includes the following:

- Not coming when called
- Staying out of reach
- Inattention to owner

Alert!
I mean it. If your dog is displaying the early warning signs of anxiety, fear, escape, and avoidance, do not wait any longer to fix them using positive methods. If you increase your punishment to try to correct the problem, you may as well cash it in now. Be sure your homeowner's insurance is paid up because this dog will most likely become a danger to you and others.

Avoidance, whether it's active or passive, is probably one of the most widely used reactions to punishment. Dogs do it, humans do it, and maybe even the birds and bees do it. For those of us (and I include dogs in that list) who hate confrontation, avoidance is the way to go. Dogs have all sorts of rituals linked to avoiding conflict. The calming signals that dogs send to each other are all about avoiding aggression and "arguments." If you see your dog "blowing you off," look to yourself — did you raise your voice in anger or make a loud and sudden movement or noise? Did something happen in the environment that stressed him? For some dogs, any kind of change — a new person, a new piece of furniture or even a new rug, can be stressful. I promise you, he is not being "dominant" or "disobedient"—avoidance is how dogs often deal with the unknown.

As the punishment in their lives increases, escape and avoidance behaviors are the last maneuvers dogs use before aggression starts. This is the last level the dog can try before your problems really shoot through the roof. Start positive training now to regain your dog's trust.

Aggression

Aggression can be a learned behavior. That's hard to comprehend sometimes, and we may want to try to justify and explain away the aggression by saying, "Well, what do you expect from a (insert name of breed here)?" That only gets rid of any guilt or denial you may feel; it doesn't help you solve the problem that punishment caused.

The breed of dog may have nothing to do with aggression. Yes, there are some breeds that were specifically bred to do certain jobs requiring force, but bad training methods are bad training methods. Period. Answer aggression with aggression, and think you'll get a happy, well-adjusted dog? Think again! I've worked with many of the so-called "aggressive" breeds and found them to be wonderfully smart, sweet, and teachable.

Some of the more obvious signs of aggression are the following:

- Growling
- Biting
- Snarling
- Snapping
- Attacking

When I come across a dog who growls at me, I get down and kiss his feet (well, not literally) and thank him for warning me. Punish the dog for giving off a warning and guess what? You won't get warnings anymore—you'll just get a bite.

Types and Causes of Aggression

There are many, many causes of aggression, and most of them can be corrected. For example, some people who own aggressive dogs may deliberately encourage the dog because they enjoy the feeling of power or of feeling protected.

Here is the short list of causes:

1. Territoriality

2. Putting animals in a position to feel vulnerable to attack by other dogs (such as forcing their heads away by the use of head halters)

3. Influx of new members to the household (canine or human)

4. Resource guarding—can be food, objects, or humans

5. Hormonal—normal seasonal fluctuations, such as breeding, arousal level, or cycling females

6. Physical stress—injury, illness, drugs, reactions to collars or corrections

7. Responses to punishment

8. Scheduled induced aggression—incorrect use of a reinforcement schedule

9. Our responses to aggression—reinforcement, whether accidental or intentional

Although punishment (from humans) may initially suppress aggressive behaviors, dogs learn to mask the early observable (to humans) aggressive signals in order to avoid punishment. Punishment can actually lead to and cause a variety of negative manifestations, including aggression.

Remember when I said aggression may be a learned behavior? Aggression, from the dog's point of view, keeps the animal safe from danger. If a scary thing appears out of nowhere and startles the dog, the dog aggresses, and the scary thing either goes away or the owner takes the dog away. The aggressive behavior therefore "worked" and will be repeated the next time the dog is afraid.

Details

Buddy lived in a household with three other dogs. When a fifth dog was brought in, Buddy did an about-face in behavior. Even though he used to be a "doggie diplomat"—very gentle and nice to strange dogs—he became fearful and would growl and snap at other dogs.

What happened? It turns out that the fifth dog was aggressive toward Buddy, and Buddy was showing redirected aggression to other dogs. Once the fifth dog was managed better and the punishing stopped, Buddy went back to being his normal, sweet self.

And was the fifth dog punished? No way! He was heavily reinforced for presenting friendly behavior, and soon stopped bullying Buddy on his own!

Learned Helplessness

Increase your punishment so much so that the dog no longer has any other recourse or alternatives to protect himself and you'll create learned helplessness. Some of the signs are the following:

- Cowering
- Rolling over
- Submission
- Eyes glazed over
- Motionless (can be frozen in a submissive posture)
- Appearing catatonic or deaf

Behavioral science shows us that continual use of inescapable punishment teaches the dog (and humans) to do literally nothing—to be helpless. As the punishment escalates, the level of intensity of the dog's reactions will increase from anxiety right up to learned helplessness. If the intensity of the punishment is so high with no escape possible, all mammals will go into learned helplessness.

Efforts to prod him into action will most likely be ineffectual. Even when presented with further punishment, the dog will do nothing further to avoid the punishment, and will just endure quietly whatever additional castigation you dole out.

I hope I have convinced you to cease and desist any and all punishments. I don't care what behavior problem you have; punishment is never warranted.

Pop Quiz

1. What does your dog find punishing?

2. What are the six observable effects of punishment?

3. Have you noticed lately any of the signs of anxiety in your dog?

Summary

Causes of "bad" behaviors can include punishment from humans, other dogs, and the environment.

Punishment only makes us feel better; it does nothing to stop "bad" behaviors.

Punishment creates more problems, such as anxiety, fear, escape, avoidance, aggression, and learned helplessness.

Incorporating Training into Your Life 17

I'm sure you're wondering how the heck you're supposed to train your dog when you work full-time. With a little planning on your part, you can easily accomplish it. The charts and tips in this chapter will show you the way. Then you'll get a preview of some of the fun training activities that you and your dog can participate in down the road.

When athletes train, they are consistent and dedicated. They know that if they put off training, they'll lose their skills. Dog training is not like riding a bike—your dog will forget his new behaviors if they aren't practiced. Take a break and you will lose the momentum and desire to continue.

While you do have to consistently set aside some time almost each and every day to spend some quality time training your friend, you should vary the frequency and type of reinforcement given during those sessions. But don't confuse "consistency in training" with being variable and unpredictable in how you reinforce.

Creating Creative Training Sessions

If it's hard for you to be creative in how you set up your training sessions, try this: write five to 10, or more behaviors on separate slips of paper. Here are some examples of desirable behaviors to use:

Make different slips for each behavior and include for no distractions, mild distractions, and lots of distractions

- Sit
- Backups
- Sit stay (10 and 20 seconds)
- Down
- Loose-leash walking (with no distractions, mild distractions, and lots of distractions)
- Down stay (10 and 20 seconds)
- Shake paw
- Sit politely for petting (by you and by someone else)
- Roll over
- Settle (with and without handling)
- Door etiquette in the house, car, and vet's office

- Come (with no distractions, mild distractions, and lots of distractions)
- Stand
- Heeling games

Fold up the slips and put them in a hat. Every day, pick three behaviors out of the hat and that's what you work on for that day. At the end of the day, put those slips back into the hat to be used again.

You can do the same thing with your list of reinforcers. Pick a few out of the hat and those are how you'll reinforce your dog for that session. As your dog's skill level goes up, exchange the slips for more difficult behaviors. These don't have to be all that complicated—just pick things that will stimulate his brain. Here are a few examples:

- Hide a treat or toy in a blanket or towel and encourage the dog to "find it." This encourages him to use his nose—great for scent-discrimination exercises for more advanced training.

- Show him a toy, tell him to stay, and then hide the toy (in plain sight at first). Then release him to "find it." You can gradually make your hiding places harder and harder.

- Teach him to touch his nose to a target—such as your hand or a plastic lid. Nose targeting is great for many things—it teaches the dog to turn his head away from another dog to avoid potential problems (head turning is a calming signal). Targeting a plastic lid is great for when you're teaching some of the obstacles in agility training.

- Get a Kong toy and fill it with gooey things and some hard treats that are slightly bigger than the opening. This will give him a little mental puzzle to keep him happy and busy.

- Use dog puzzles — see appendix for the link.

There are many simple ways to add enrichment and variability to your dog's life without going too crazy. You can even teach him service-dog behaviors, such as picking up keys—or better yet—finding keys, closing cabinet doors (I wouldn't recommend teaching him to open cabinet doors), or retrieving your slippers. I recently taught Emma to retrieve the phone for me in case of an emergency. She is so proud of herself, as she should be! Side note: I did not teach all of my dogs to do this because I didn't want them fighting over the phone when it counts. And I keep the base taped to the nightstand and never use that phone, so it's always in the same place.

Training Goals

No one is ever done with training, but there are some basic behaviors you should strive for, as recommended by noted positive trainer Ted Turner. All of these behaviors are taught in previous chapters. Teach them and you will be the envy of every other dog owner you meet!

- Eye contact
- Name recognition
- Praise-word recognition
- Walking on a loose leash
- Attention heeling
- Accepting petting, handling, and grooming
- Stays (with distractions)
- Recall (with distractions)
- Crate training
- Control in and out of doorways and cars
- Potty training
- Ignoring dropped food
- No aggression to humans or dogs
- No jumping, mouthing, or biting
- Tolerance of children
- Not totally reliant on food as a reinforcer

Please don't think that these are unattainable—they aren't. It just takes consistency, patience, specific goals on your part, and faith that your dog—yes, your dog—can achieve this level of training.

Incorporating Training into Your Routine

I know it's hard sometimes to think about training your dog when you come home tired, but you owe it to yourself and to your dog. After all, why else did you get a dog if not to have fun with him? Once you "just do it," you should find that your energy level actually increases and your mental state improves. It has been proven that when hospital or nursing-home patients are around dogs, they're happier and more relaxed.

> **Alert!**
> When running errands while training your dog, be sure to watch the weather. In even relatively mild weather (65 degrees and above), a dog can die of heatstroke in six minutes if left in a closed and unprotected car. Even if he doesn't die, he can suffer irreparable brain damage.

You can train your dog almost any time of the day or night—while you cook, eat, clean, talk on the phone, work on the computer, watch TV, run errands, go to the softball game, go swimming, take a hike, or ride a bike.

A typical day of running errands and training at the same time can be the following:

• Go to the bank, bring the dog with you, and practice door etiquette.

• Pick up your dry cleaning and practice loose-leash walking in the parking lot.

• While doing your laundry at the Laundromat, practice stays and eye contact, and play the "hide the cookie" or "toy in the towel" game. You can even put the dog on a longer leash and practice recalls.

• When you go to the pet supply shop, practice door etiquette, sitting politely for petting, and loose-leash walking.

So you see, it's not hard to find time to work with your dog. My hope for you is that you become a training junkie and sell your couch and TV to make room for training equipment!

An Apple a Day

If you spend as little as three five-minute sessions per day training your dog, you'll have a good dog. The sessions don't have to be strictly formal—you can train your dog while running errands or doing chores around the house. You can (and should) train while you play with him and play while you train. Your dog should not know the difference between playing and training—both should be equally fun and satisfying. What may actually happen is that you end up enjoying the sessions because your dog soaks up whatever you teach him. You'll see positive results in the day-to-day behavior of your dog, and that will spur you on to train more.

Following the training charts in this section will …

> • Keep you on track with each new behavior.
> • Advance each behavior in small approximations (steps).
> • Help you to become variable in how you reinforce.
> • Give you an idea of how to train your dog, even while cleaning the house.

Sample Training Guides

These charts are a checklist and guideline for training. They list the many different behaviors you can work on, plus how you can be variable and unpredictable in how you reinforce each repetition. Once you get the hang of this, you can make up your own charts based on the behaviors your dog still needs to learn.

> *Details*
> Bobbi grumbled about one of the charts that showed how to train while cleaning. Her complaint? "But that means I have to clean!"

WEEK ONE

Monday

Session 1   Sit
___ 2 treats
___ 5 treats
___ pets & praise
___ 1 treat & pet
___ ball toss

Backups
___ 10 treats
___ 1 treat
___ ball toss
___ 4 treats
___ pets & praise
___ 6 treats

Eye Contact
___ 1 treat
___ 4 treats
___ pets & praise
___ 2 treats
___ 1 treat
___ run away silly
___ 4 treats

Session 2
Come, click & treat
For 5 minutes

Sit
___ 2 treats
___ 3 treats
___ pet & 1 treat
___ praise
___ 5 treats

Eye Contact
___ 1 treat
___ 2 treats
___ ball toss
___ praise
___ petting
___ 5 treats

Tuesday
Down
___ 10 treats
___ pet and 2 treats
___ ball toss
___ 1 treat
___ 4 treats

Eye contact
___ pets & praise
___ 3 treats
___ 1 treat
___ pet & ball toss
___ 1 treat
___ 1 treat

Sit
___ praise
___ 1 treat
___ ball toss
___ run away silly
___ 2 treats
___ 1 treat
___ pet

Backups
___ 1 treat
___ 1 treat
___ 6 treats
___ run away silly
___ 2 treats
___ pets & praise

Come, click & treat
for 2 minutes

Down
___ 5 treats
___ 2 treats
___ pets & praise
___ pets & 8 treats
___ pets and water

Wednesday
Eye contact
___ 1 treat
___ 2 treats
___ pets & praise
___ pet & 1 treat
___ 1 treat

Name, click, treat
For 5 minutes

Cuddle time

Down
___ 9 treats
___ ball toss
___ 3 treats
___ run away silly

Sit
___ praise
___ Praise and pets
___ 4 treats
___ 1 treat

Sit before you throw the toy.

Down before you throw the toy.

Name, click & treat for 5 minutes

Backups
___ 1 treat
___ 1 treat
___ 4 treats

Thursday
Cuddle time

Come, click & treat
For 5 minutes

Name, click & treat for 5 minutes

Sit for toy tosses

Down for toy tosses

Eye contact for toy tosses

Stand
___ 1 treat
___ 2 treats
___ 1 treat
___ 5 treats

Cuddle time

Eye contact for petting

Sit
___ 1 treat
___ hand clapping
___ run away silly
___ ball toss
___ 4 treats

Friday
Stand
___ 3 treats
___ gentle petting
___ 5 treats

Eye contact, click & treat for 3 minutes

Put leash on, click and treat. Then take leash off, click and treat – repeat 10 times

Backups
___ 4 treats
___ petting
___ Praise
___ 7 treats
___ 1 treat

Hide & Seek – praise, treats and petting
___ in the bathroom
___ in the bedroom
___ in the closet
___ in the kitchen

Touch top of head game – repeat 10 times, clicking & treating for no movement away

Cuddle time

Saturday
Go to a field and play with dog on a 50-foot long line

While playing, add in:

Eye contact, click & treat for 2 minutes

Name, click & treat for 3 minutes

3 sits
___ 3 treats
___ petting
___ 1 treat

4 downs
___ petting
___ praise
___ 5 treats

Backups
___ 6 treats
___ praise
___ 1 treat
___ ball toss

Once at home, Put leash on, click and treat. Then take leash off, click and treat – repeat 10 times

Touch top of head and neck areas – repeat 10 times, clicking & treating for no movement away.

WEEK TWO

Monday

Session 1   **Sit**
— 1 treats
— 7 treats
— pets & praise
— 1 treat & pet
— ball toss

Stand stay
— 1 second
— 2 seconds
— 3 seconds
— 4 seconds
— 5 seconds
— 6 seconds

Eye Contact
— 1 treat
— 1 treat
— pets & praise
— 2 treats
— 1 treat
— run away silly
— 4 treats

Come, click & treat
For 5 minutes

Stand w/touching
— 1 treats
— 2 treats
— pet & 1 treat
— praise
— 5 treats

Name, click & treat
for 2 minutes

Tuesday

Down
— 10 treats
— pet and 2 treats
— ball toss
— 1 treat
— 4 treats

Down stay
— 3 seconds
— 3 seconds
play for 4 minutes

Down stay
— 3 seconds
— 8 seconds
— 4 seconds

Sit
— praise
— 1 treat
— ball toss
— run away silly
— 4 treats
— pet & 3 treats
— pet

Backups w/ distractions
— 4 treats
— 2 treat
— 6 treats
— run away silly
— 2 treats
— pets & praise

Come, click & treat
for 2 minutes

Wednesday

Throw the cookie game
— 10 treats
— 12 treats
— pets & praise
— pet & 1 treat
— 7 treats

Down stay
— 4 seconds
— 6 seconds
— 10 seconds

Name, click, treat
For 5 minutes

Stand for touching
— 4 treats
— 3 treats
— 5 treats

Sit for toy tosses

Eye contact for toy tosses

Sit
— praise
— Praise and pets
— 4 treats
— 1 treat
— run away silly

Practice door etiquette

Practice food bowl etiquette

Name, click & treat for 5 minutes

Thursday

Eye contact
— 1 treat
— petting
— praise
— 8 treats

Come, click & treat
For 5 minutes

Throw the cookie game
— 6 treats
— 8 treats
— 10 treats
— petting & 11 treats

Cuddle time

Down stay
— 6 seconds
— 10 seconds
— 15 seconds

Eye contact for toy tosses

Stand stay
— 1 treat
— 2 treats
— 1 treat
— 5 treats

Cuddle time

Eye contact for petting

Put leash on, click and treat. Then take leash off, click and treat – repeat 10 times

Friday

Sit stays
— 10 seconds
— 18 seconds
— 18 seconds

Eye contact, click & treat for 3 minutes

Put leash on, click and treat. Then take leash off, click and treat – repeat 10 times

Backups w/ distractions
— 4 treats
— petting
— run away silly
— 7 treats
— 1 treat

Hide & Seek – praise, treats and petting
— in the bathroom
— in the bedroom
— in the closet
— in the kitchen

Touch top of head game – repeat 10 times, clicking & treating for no movement away

Cuddle time

Play fetch for eye contact, sits and downs

Saturday

Go to a field and play with dog on a 50-foot long line

While playing, add in:

The two toy game and the two tug game. Be sure to play by your rules.

Name, click & treat for 3 minutes

Backups or perhaps loose leash walking if your dog is focused on you.

Teach your dog how to shake paw

Pivot to heel
— 5 steps
— 10 steps
— 8 steps

Once at home, Put leash on, click and treat. Then take leash off, click and treat – repeat 10 times

Cuddle time

WEEK THREE

Monday

Drop the cookie game
— 1 treat
— 7 treats
— pets & praise
— 2 tug game
— 4 treats

Heeling
— 1 step (C/T)
— 5 steps (C/T)
— 8 steps (C/T)
— 12 steps (C/T)
— 3 steps (C/T)
— 20 steps (C/T)

Down stay
— 35 seconds
— 40 seconds
— 20 seconds

Practice "Shake paw"

Cuddle time

Name, click & treat for 3 minutes

Food bowl etiquette

Water bowl etiquette

Sit
— 4 treats
— 1 treat
— petting
— praise

Tuesday

Door etiquette
— front door
— back door
— side door

Down stay
— 20 seconds

play for 5 minutes

Stand stay for petting
— head
— shoulder
— back
— head

Sit
— praise
— 1 treat
— ball toss
— run away silly
— 4 treats
— pet & 3 treats
— pet

Loose leash walking
— 1 step (C/T)
— 2 steps (C/T)
— 3 steps (C/T)
— 8 steps (C/T)
— 10 steps (C/T)
— 2 steps (C/T)

Have someone hold your dogs leash, while you call the dog. Make sure they drop the leash as soon as you say "come." As reinforcers, use food, petting, praise, run away silly and toys

Wednesday

Real Life
— 2 toy game while dusting
— down stay while doing dishes
— down stay while vacuuming
— throw the cookie game while working on computer

Loose leash walking
— 3 steps (C/T)
— 4 steps (C/T)
— 6 steps (C/T)
— 2 steps (C/T)
— 8 steps (C/T)

Name, click, treat For 5 minutes

Door etiquette
— in the car
— coming out of car
— at the post office
— at the bank
— at the laundromat

Cuddle time

Teach your dog to "wave" Bonus points if you teach the dog to shake and wave with both paws!

Settle
— 5 treats
— 3 treats
— 4 treats
— 1 treat
— run away silly

Thursday

Settle
— 1 treat
— light petting
— 3 treats
— 6 treats

Name, click & treat For 5 minutes

Drop the cookie game
— petting
— praise & 8 treats
— 6 treats
— petting & 3 treats

Settle with a stay
— 9 treats
— 3 treats
— 1 treat
— light petting
— 5 treats

Down stay
— 20 seconds
— 35 seconds

Sits for toy tosses

Stand stay
— for paw touches
— for paw touches
— for head touch
— for leaning over in an obnoxious way

Eye contact for petting & toy toss

Put leash on, click and treat. Then take leash off, click and treat – repeat 10 times

Friday

Teach your dog to roll over

Name, click & treat for 3 minutes

Stand stay
— for head touch
— for tail touch
— for paw touch

Loose leash walking
— 4 steps (C/T)
— 5 steps (C/T)
— 5 steps (C/T)
— 5 steps (C/T)
— 5 steps (C/T)

2 tug game – don't forget the rules! Add in a sit or down before allowing the dog to retake the toy.

Sit stay
— 20 seconds
— 15 seconds
— 30 seconds

Cuddle time

Sit still while you brush for treats. Keep it slow – 1 brush stroke at a time. Continue in this vein, adding more and more brushing. Have someone help you by feeding it dog is still.

Saturday

Show off to your friends all you have taught your dog in ONLY 3 weeks! Congratulations!!!

Loose leash walking for 5 steps

Sit

Down

Down stay

Stand & stay for handling

Shake paw and wave

Settle

Roll over

Name recognition

Come word recognition

Door etiquette

Staying still for petting

Not leaving you even if the leash is off, until you release the dog

Fetch games for eye contact, sits and downs

As you can see, this is all pretty basic stuff that will fit easily into your busy schedule. You'll notice that, in the beginning, lots of food is used, but as the weeks go on, other types of reinforcers are used to keep the behaviors intact.

Where All This Fun Might Lead You

Okay, so now you're completely and utterly hooked on dog training. Your dog is performing incredible behaviors and you want more! Good for you—and great for your dog! Never fear, there are plenty of additional activities you can do with your dog.

Therapy Dog

Most hospitals, nursing homes, and schools welcome Therapy Dogs. The primary objective for a Therapy Dog is to provide comfort and companionship to patients. The dogs increase emotional well-being, promote healing, and improve the quality of life for the people they visit.

> ### *Detail*
> Many years ago, I took my Sheltie, Noel, to a nursing home. One time, a nurse asked me if I could put Noel in bed with a woman who had been comatose for many years. When I did, the nurse took the woman's hand and had her gently pet Noel. Within seconds there was a definite positive reaction from the patient. We all cried.

For your dog to be a registered Therapy Dog, he must first pass his Canine Good Citizen (CGC) test (see Chapter 18), as well as be trained to ignore dropped food (not really as hard as you may think!) and be calm around wheelchairs, walkers, and canes. In addition, the dog needs to be relaxed around people walking erratically and be willing to be handled by strangers and to actively seek out petting. Your dog must be at least one year old to take the test.

There are many organizations that you can register with to enable your dog to become a Therapy Dog. They generally offer insurance (in case your dog accidentally hurts someone) that is usually inexpensive. The Delta Society and Therapy Dog International are the two largest organizations. If your dog is not registered with a group, you will not be allowed to enter hospitals or nursing homes with him.

Rally

This is a sport that's a natural stepping-stone from the CGC to competition obedience or agility (see the following sections for more on these dog sports). Many of the maneuvers are similar to competition obedience, but you can talk to your dog the entire time while giving extra cues. You follow a course of signs and do the behavior listed on the sign, rather than respond to a judge's commands as you would in competition obedience.

World Cynosport Rally, American Kennel Club and ASCA (Australian Shepherd Club of America) offers titles in Rally for all breeds and mixed breeds.

Competition Obedience

Competition obedience is the foundation upon which all other dog sports are based. Training for competition develops a strong working relationship between the dog and his owner. A few of the behaviors your dog must master to earn the three main titles are heeling on and off leash at different paces, standing still while a stranger lightly examines the dog, "Sit/Stay" and "Down/Stay" in a group of other dogs, dumbbell retrieves, jumping, and scent discrimination.

There are three main levels of obedience competition: Novice, Open, and Utility. You can also train for and earn an Obedience Trial Champion (OTCH) title. The levels increase in complexity and really hones your skills as a trainer. Any one of the titles says a great deal about you and your dog, your relationship, and your dedication. Your dog can wear these titles proudly.

There are three main registries that promote competition obedience. The AKC, United Kennel Club (UKC) and Australian Shepherd Club of America (ASCA) all allow any breed as well as mixed breeds to compete in its trials.

Competition Obedience

Agility

Very simply, agility is an obstacle course for dogs. Your dog must follow the course correctly, accurately, safely, and fast! There are many levels and types of classes offered that will fit into most people's and dog's abilities.

Agility is fun and challenging to both dog and handler. The AKC offers agility trials as do the North American Agility Council (NADAC) and United States Dog Agility Association (USDAA).

Agility

Many people may think competition obedience or Rally is too hard and may want to skip right to Agility. Granted, Agility may seem like more fun, but you really can't do Agility without basic obedience. After all, your dog will be off leash while other dogs and people are outside the ring, and you will need to know that your dog will stay with you. So while you can do competition obedience without Agility, you can't do Agility without obedience!

Sheep Herding

You can train for sheep herding with just about any breed of dog that has any "sheep sense." I've even seen Standard Poodles and German Shorthaired Pointers do a fine job herding sheep. However, if you want to actually compete, you can do so only with a breed of dog that the AKC classifies as part of the Herding group (for example, Border Collies, Old English Sheepdogs, and Corgis). The AKC and ASCA are the two registries that hold herding trials. There are also many trials for Border Collies only.

Sheep Herding
Photo: B.P. Mitchell

Musical Freestyle

Musical freestyle is "dancing with your dog" to music. Many of the behaviors you can use are fun and funny. The great thing about freestyle is that the only limitations are your own imagination. If you have even a slight sense of rhythm (I don't, but I still like to train the behaviors), like music, and like to be creative, then freestyle is for you. Many people aren't interested in competing for titles, but use their routines for demos at pet fairs or at nursing homes, or at the very least to amaze and impress their friends. You don't need any special equipment and it is a great sport to practice on those rainy days. World Canine Freestyle Organization (WCFO) even offers the ability to compete for titles via videotape.

Musical Freestyle
Photo: M. Mustich

Treibball

Treibball, a new sport from Germany — also called ball herding or soccer for dogs is an amazingly fun sport for both dog and handler. Essentially, you stand in a specified area and direct your dog out from 15-25 feet to bring back the balls, one at a time. The beginning levels starts with three balls and the upper level has eight balls. All breeds and mixed breeds are welcome. NATE (National Association of Treibball Enthusiasts) is one organization that holds matches (practice shows) and trials.

Treibball
Photo: C. Stearns

Nosework

Inspired by working detection dogs, K9 Nose Work is a fun search and scenting activity for virtually all dogs and people. This easy to learn activity and sport builds confidence and focus in many dogs, and provides a safe way to keep dogs fit and healthy through mental and physical exercise. All dogs are welcome. NACSW (National Association of Canine Scent Work) holds trials.

Other Sports

There are additional dog sports for many other breeds, such as tracking, search and rescue, carting (pulling a cart), weight pull, flyball (a timed relay race, with a team of four dogs jumping over four hurdles, taking a tennis ball out of a "flyball box," and jumping back over the four hurdles), earthdog (or "go to ground," where terriers find safely caged rodents underground), Barn Hunt (where the dog has to find one to three hidden, contained rats through a maze of hay bales, Canine Water Sports (all breeds and mixed), lure coursing (chasing a "lure" through a prescribed course), conformation (a beauty contest for purebred dogs—think "Westminster Kennel Club dog show"), and water rescue. For more information, see the Appendix. Each of these sports has a personality of its own. You will meet some wonderful people and develop great new friendships, which will change your life—and your dog's life—for the better.

Although these dogs are draft dogs, any dog can learn to pull a cart.

Photo: W. Eld

Tracking win shot!

Pop Quiz

1. How many places have you taken your dog to train?

2. Have you been able to train your dog for at least three five-minute sessions per day?

3. Have you been diligent about using reinforcers other than food?

4. Have you decided which dog sport you'd like to learn more about?

Summary

Train a few minutes every day and you will have a great dog.

Use the places on your daily errand list as opportunities to train your dog.

Lay down your dog's foundation behaviors and the sky's the limit to what you can accomplish.

Get involved with some dog sports and make new friends.

The Canine Good Citizen Test   18

Using the positive methods outlined in this book, you've taught your dog all the essentials he'll need to pass the Canine Good Citizen (CGC) test. The purpose of the CGC is to ensure that your best friend will be invited back as a welcome guest wherever he goes.

Earning your CGC title says a great deal about you and your dog. It says that you took the time and effort to properly teach your dog the much-needed skills to be a respected and safe member of society and, in some instances, to enable you to get or even keep your homeowner's insurance. It also says that you took training seriously and that you understand the importance of a formal education for your four-footed friend. In short, it speaks a lot for you, too.

> ### *Detail*
> A few years ago I was looking for a new insurance company. When I called about rates, I mentioned that I had three dogs. I heard the hesitation in the operators' voice, so told her that, "All of my dog have their CGC, all have multiple obedience titles, I have a 6 foot privacy fence and I'm a dog trainer, and…" She interrupted me and said, "You got me on CGC."

The CGC test is comprised of ten sections. The first three are accepting a friendly stranger, sitting politely for petting, and appearance and grooming. The following sections explore what you'll need to practice for each part of the test.

Accepting a Friendly Stranger

Your dog is to be at your side, preferably sitting or lying down. The tester approaches and the dog should remain in position, or at the very least, should not jump on the tester. The tester shakes hands with you and does not interact with your dog. You may talk to your dog, and remind him to stay. The best way to teach this is to teach your dog that "a person approaching is a cue to sit." The instructions for that are in chapter 15.

A dog accepting a friendly stranger.

Photo: T. Hirsch

Sitting Politely for Petting

This exercise is almost the same as the first one. The idea is to get the dog used to people petting him without him getting upset or jumping. The tester will approach your dog. The dog should be in either a "Sit" or a "Down." The tester then lightly pets your dog. Once your dog has learned to remain seated while someone approaches, training for this one is a piece of cake. Follow these steps:

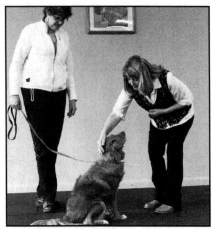

Dog accepting petting
Photo: T. Hirsch

1. Have the stranger approach your dog while you remind your dog to sit.

2. As the stranger reaches out to pet your dog, feed your dog a treat. As soon as the petting stops, stop feeding the treats.

3. Have the person walk away and then walk back and do it again.

4. After about five to six times, you shouldn't need to feed your dog because he is now comfortable with a stranger petting him.

5. Change your stranger to a new person and repeat all of the preceding steps.

If at any time your dog jumps, don't yank him down. Don't forget that opposition reflex causes the dog to push or pull against anything that is pushing or pulling against him. So of course, the more you yank on your dog, the more he will jump.

Appearance and Grooming

This test demonstrates that your dog will accept handling from a stranger, such as a groomer or veterinarian. The tester approaches your dog, lightly brushes him (just a few strokes), lifts up and examines each front foot, and touches each ear. When training, break this exercise into three parts: brushing, foot lifting, and then ear touching. Here's what to do:

> ***Alert!***
> Make sure your dog is comfortable with you doing these things before having your stranger do them. Review Chapter 7 to make sure that your dog is perfectly relaxed about being handled in this way.

Taking the last set of steps, you can now add in brushing along with the touching of each body part. Remember to go slow so as not to distress your dog.

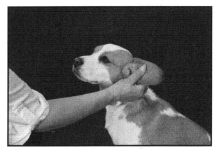

Accepting ear touches.
Photo: T. Hirsch

Aceepting paw touches
Photo: T. Hirsch

When your dog is comfortable with strangers brushing him, repeat all of the preceding steps but insert paw lifting after the brushing. After he's doing well with his feet being touched, you can add ear touches.

If you practice these three sections religiously, your dog will breeze through them come test time.

> ***Pointer***
> The obvious benefit to these exercises is that your dog will welcome petting and handling by strangers and not need to be muzzled for grooming and vet visits.

Heeling/Loose leash walking; Out for a walk

Sections four and five of the test have to do with loose-leash walking. Review Chapter 8 and make sure you've taken it "on the road" and proofed loose-leash walking and heeling in all kinds of strange places before you take the test.

The dog doesn't have to be in rigid "heel" position, because this is not competition obedience. Although when I take my dogs to be tested, I have them heel. The tester just needs to see that the dog is attentive to you and will stay with you if you change direction. You'll be directed to lead your dog in a right turn, a left turn, and an about turn (a 180-degree turnaround), with a stop in between and one at the end. Don't forget that you can talk to your dog and encourage him to follow you as you make each turn.

In section four, "out for a walk" demonstrates that you can walk your dog on a loose leash and that he doesn't walk you. He may be on either your right or left side, whichever you prefer. The dog doesn't need to sit when you stop, but it helps in keeping his attention.

If the leash is pulled tight continually or the dog sniffs the ground excessively, the dog will not pass the test. Be sure to practice using the other types of reinforcers listed in Chapter 12, because food or toys are not allowed during the CGC test.

Walking Through a Crowd

Test five shows that your dog can walk politely in a crowd of people without jumping on them or ripping your shoulder out of its socket. Your dog can show some interest in the crowd, but must continue to walk with you. Sniffing a person briefly is allowed, but the dog should come back to you and proceed with your walk.

Because you've done your homework, this should be pretty easy for you and your dog. If you're still having problems with this, don't despair. Just practice more, continuing to make it fun for your dog to ignore people. Heavily reinforce with petting, food, and toys when he leaves strangers alone.

Walking through a crowd.
Photo: T. Hirsch

Sit, down, stay

Tests six and seven show that the dog has training and will respond to your cues of "Sit," "Down," and "Stay." Because you've practiced this in many different contexts, this will be a walk in the park for you (pun intended).

The tester will ask you to have your dog do a "Sit" or "Down." As you already learned, you don't need to push or pull the dog into position, and these methods are not allowed during the test anyway.

Prior to this test, a 20-foot lead is attached to the dog's collar. After the dog does the "Sit" and "Down," you will be instructed to ask the dog to "Stay." You can do either a "Sit/Stay" or a "Down/Stay"—whichever your dog does better. Then you walk out to the end of the 20-foot line, turn around, and come right back. You can say "Stay, stay, stay" the entire time. You won't need to if you've trained properly, but if it makes you feel better, you can repeat the cues.

> ***Pointer***
> You can talk to your dog incessantly throughout the test. In fact, I recommend talking to your dog to relax both of you.

Coming When Called

This test demonstrates that the dog will come when called. While the dog is still on the 20-foot line, you will walk 10 feet away from him, telling him to "Wait" or "Stay." Then you call your dog to you. You can use thigh slapping or verbal encouragement and can call the dog numerous times. However, you won't have to because you've trained him to respond on the first cue!

Reaction to Distractions

Tests eight and nine show that your dog won't have a fearful or aggressive reaction to distractions or other dogs. A Good Citizen is not just about being good around human strangers, but around dog strangers as well.

There are two types of distractions used during test eight: a visual one and an audible one. The tester might use a person on crutches, a walker, or a wheelchair; the sudden opening or closing of a door; a jogger or bicyclist; a person pushing a shopping cart; or someone clanging metal bowls or dropping a large book.

To train for these things, start with the audible distractions. Set up your sessions carefully, and gradually make the distractions bigger. Here's what you should do:

1. Start with a small paperback book and drop it on the floor while feeding the dog simultaneously.

2. Repeat a few times to ensure that the dog has no reaction.

3. Graduate to a larger book and repeat steps 1 and 2.

Provided that the dog didn't react to the books, you can now add something a little noisier, like a metal bowl or pan. Continue to feed him simultaneously while dropping the objects. When training this, be sure to not drop the objects right next to or behind your dog.

> *Alert!*
> Your dog is permitted to show a casual interest in the noise or sight distractions, but he can't show fear, resentment, or shyness. He can even startle slightly, but must not try to pull away in fear. He also has to show that he can recover from the startle within a short period of time and not remain shaking or cowering.
>
> Obviously, urinating or defecating in fear, or barking and lunging, are not acceptable. A few barks may be all right if the dog is then silent.

Persevere in training using more and louder noises, always making sure that you feed your dog for calm behaviors. If at any time your dog shows nervousness or fear, move back a step and reinforce at the last level he was successful. Then move up the ladder at a slower rate.

Now you can add visual distractions. Start back at the beginning, using a mild one, such as a kid's wheelbarrow or even someone walking a bicycle. As you did with audible distractions, add bigger items that are moving faster and faster.

> *Pointer*
> As the distraction passes by, you're allowed to remind your dog to stay. Don't underestimate the power of the "Stay." If a dog is slightly nervous, responding to a cue from you may just help him relax; it gives him a "job" to do.

Reaction to Another Dog

Passing test nine is another sure sign that you've done a fantastic job training your dog. Another handler and neutral dog will approach you and your dog. When you're within arm's length of each other, you will all stop and you will ask your dog to sit or lie down.

You and the other handler will shake hands and exchange pleasantries for a few seconds and then move away from each other. The dogs will be on the outside (left) of the handlers as they approach each other. Your dog can show a mild interest in the other dog, but must show no fear, shyness, aggression, panic, or "Hi there, let's dump these humans and go play!"

> *Details*
> If the distraction dog creates a ruckus, you can ask to take that portion of the test again with a more appropriate dog. You are entitled to a "neutral" dog.

You can teach your dog to accept a neutral dog the same way you taught him to accept a friendly stranger. Take it in small steps, heavily reinforcing your dog for remaining calm around the other dog. I like to start with two dogs, walking far apart and parallel to each other (walking parallel is a calming signal). Once your dog is comfortable, gradually come in a little closer. Once you are walking almost side by side, you can now start walking toward each other. Start out far away and gradually come in closer and closer.

Two dogs walking parallel to each other with handlers in between.

Photo: T. Hirsch

Two dogs and their handlers approaching, stopping and shaking hands. Both dogs are quite at ease next to their handlers.

Photo: T. Hirsch

Supervised separation

Supervised separation is the last and sometimes the hardest section of the CGC test. This test shows that your dog can be left alone for three minutes with a stranger and maintain his good manners and training. The dog doesn't have to stay in position, but isn't allowed to jump on the evaluator or otherwise be a pest. The dog is not permitted to whine, bark, howl, growl, pace, or show anything more than mild agitation.

Training for supervised separation need not be traumatic for your dog. Just as with everything else in positive training, break it down into tiny approximations and you'll have a dog who doesn't freak out if you leave him.

> ### Alert!
> If the test is held outside, urinating or defecating is allowed for only this test. If, however, the test is held indoors, either action is an immediate cause for failure.

> ### Detail
> This seemingly useless test is actually a fantastic experience for your dog. We don't like to think about it, but what would happen to your dog if something happened to you? Would he be able to move nicely and serenely into a new home, or would he freak out at being away from you?
>
> Although having a great relationship with your dog is essential, you also want your dog to be able to be with other people. At the very least, I'm sure you'd like to go on vacation without your dog being traumatized.

To train for supervised separation, follow these steps:

1. Start out with a friend whom the dog knows and likes.

2. Go out of sight for three seconds. Have your friend feed the dog a few treats while you're gone.

3. When you come back, don't go crazy with praise; soft petting and praise will be sufficient.

4. Leave again for five seconds while your friend feeds the dog.

Be sure to use a timer when you practice this so that you don't inadvertently leave for too long. Continue adding a few seconds more each time until you gradually build up to three minutes of your dog being calm without you.

Your friend should also start feeding less once you've reached the full three minutes. If at any time your dog gets nervous, have your friend try to redirect to simple behaviors such as a "Sit" or "Down." He or she can also try some of the calming signals such as yawning or lip licking. Be sure that the friend doesn't inadvertently reinforce your dog for being nervous by talking, petting, or comforting him.

Above all, do not rush this. If your dog gets too nervous, you don't want to come back to him, because then he learns that his nervousness brings you back. You want him to learn that his calmness is what brings you back.

Keep your comings and goings low-key. Although it's good for your ego when your dog goes ballistic in greeting you (even if you leave for only five seconds), it's not healthy for the dog. Practice building for a few extra minutes more than you'll need. Most competition trainers teach their dogs to do the stay exercises for longer than needed. For instance, they will train a two-minute "Sit/Stay" rather than the one minute needed in the ring. Why? Because when they are really competing, it will be easier for the dog.

Practice these exercises in many locations and you'll ace your test. I also recommend that you watch a CGC test without your dog along, so that you'll know what to expect once he's ready. You'll learn the flow of the tests and how they're handled, and it will help your stress level remain low. Prepare yourself, prepare your dog, and then pick out a beautiful new frame and prominent location to hang your Canine Good Citizen certificate! Congratulations!

Summary
Put together the behaviors you taught your dog in previous chapters to train your dog to earn his CGC title.

Teach your dog to ignore and accept friendly strangers, other dogs, and handling.

The basic manners of "Sit," "Down," "Stay," and walking on a loose leash will take you far.

Teach your dog to be comfortable being away from you for even longer periods of time than needed for the test.

Appendix

Books and Web Resources

These are the books and websites that I recommend the most if you'd like to learn more about positive training and healthier ways to feed your dogs. I firmly believe that diet affects behavior, so I've also included some of my favorite sources addressing those issues as well.

Books and DVDs

Booth, Sheila. Purely Positive Training. Ridgefield, CT: Podium Publications, 1998.

Billinghurst, Ian. The Barf Diet. Bathurst, NSW, Australia: Warrigal Publishing, 2001.

———. Give Your Dog a Bone. Bathurst, NSW, Australia: Warrigal Publishing, 1993.

———. Grow Your Pups with Bones. Bathurst, NSW, Australia: Warrigal Publishing, 1998.

Burch, Mary R., and Jon S. Bailey. How Dogs Learn. New York: Howell Book House, 1999.

Chance, Paul. Learning and Behavior. 4th ed. Pacific Cove, Calif.: Brooks/Cole, 1999.

Dennison, Pamela S. Bringing Light to Shadow: A Dog Trainer's Diary. Wenatchee, WA: Dogwise Publishing, 2005

———. Civilizing the City Dog; A Guide to Rehabilitating Aggressive Dogs in an Urban Environment. Blairstown, NJ: Shadow Publishing, 2015

———. How to Right a Dog Gone Wrong: A Roadmap for Rehabilitating Aggressive Dogs. Blairstown, NJ: Shadow Publishing, 2015.

———. The R.E.W.A.R.D. Zone for aggressive & Reactive Dogs (DVD). Blairstown, NJ, Shadow Publishing, 2014

———. The Magic of Shaping: Explore the Possibilities. Eagle, Idaho: Tawzer Dog Videos. 2008 (DVD, 4 hour, 2 disks, menu driven, 20+ behaviors).

———. Training the Whistle Recall. Blairstown, NJ. Shadow Publishing, 2009 (DVD and whistle, 28 minutes, 5 week program, winner of the Maxwell Award for Best Training Video of 2009 from the Dog Writers Association of America)

Donaldson, Jean. The Culture Clash. Berkeley, CA: James and Kenneth Publishers, 1996.
Lorenz, Konrad. On Aggression. Translated by Marjorie Latzke. New York: Routledge, 2002.
Pitcairn, Richard H., and Susan Hubble Pitcairn. Dr. Pitcairn's Complete Guide to
Natural Health for Dogs and Cats. Emmaus, PA: Rodale Press, 1995.
Pryor, Karen. Don't Shoot the Dog. Rev. ed. New York: Bantam Books, 1999.
———. Lads Before the Wind. Waltham, Mass.: Sunshine Books, 1994.
Reid, Pamela J. Excel-erated Learning. Berkeley, CA: James and Kenneth Publishers, 1996.
Rugaas, Turid. On Talking Terms with Dogs: Calming Signals. Wenatchee, WA:
Dogwise Publishing, 1997 (book and video).
Sidman, Murray. Coercion and Its Fallout. Boston: Authors Cooperative, 1989.
Spector, Morgan. Clicker Training for Obedience. Waltham, MA: Sunshine Books, 1999.

PDF's for Trainers by Pam Dennison

Training the Whistle Recall Curriculum. Shadow Publishing, 2011, Blairstown, NJ
Are You Biting off More Than You Can Chew? Are You Really Ready to Work With
Aggression Cases? Shadow Publishing. 2014, Blairstown, NJ

Recorded webinars by Pam Dennison

Dennison, Pamela. Animal Husbandry; Helping to Create a Bomb Proof Dog
____. Loose Leash Walking
____. How to Find a Reputable Rescue Group
____. Animal Husbandry; Helping to Create a Bomb Proof Dog
____. Finding a Trainer
____. Setting Up Your Own Aggressive Dog Classes
www.pamdennison.com

Online Classes by Pam Dennison

Dennison, Pamela. You Can Train Your Dog - the companion class to this book
____. Managing the Multiple Dog Household, Part 1
____. Managing the Multiple Dog Household, Part 2
____. Cleaning Up Your Act; the fussy & meticulous behaviors needed for
competition obedience, rally and CDSP, Part 1
____. Cleaning Up Your Act; the fussy & meticulous behaviors needed for
competition obedience, rally and CDSP, Part 2
www.pamdennison.com

Websites for Training and General Dog Issues

These are my favorite websites for training and nutrition. Literally thousands of great sites are on the Internet, but there are also thousands of not-great sites. It takes a while to learn how to separate the wheat from the chaff.

Alternative Veterinary Medicine
www.altvetmed.org
Where to find a holistic veterinarian.

American Kennel Club
www.akc.org
Information about breeds, shows, CGC, and other dog sports.

Association of Professional Dog Trainers
www.apdt.com

Australian Shepherd Club of America
www.asca.org
Not just for Aussies! They allow any breed as well as mixed breeds to compete in sanctioned trials.

AVSAB position statement on puppy socialization
http://avsabonline.org/uploads/position_statements/puppy_socialization.pdf

B-Naturals www.b-naturals.com
Great source for supplements.

Black Ice
www.blackicedogsledding.com
The only source for X-back sledding harnesses—Pam's pick for the best harness for loose-leash walking!

Bluegrace Portuguese Water Dogs
www.bluegrace.com
A source for alternative medicine—not just for Portuguese Water Dogs!

Cambridge Center for Behavioral Studies
www.behavior.org
Great source for information about behavior in lay terms.

Canine Freestyle Federation, Inc.
www.canine-freestyle.org
Information about Canine Freestyle (dancing with your dog).

Canine Water Sports
www.caninewatersports.com

ClickerSolutions
www.clickersolutions.com
Loads of great information about positive training.

Delta Society
www.deltasociety.org
One of the registries for Therapy Dog work.

Dogwise.com
www.dogwise.com
Where you can get all of the books and videos/DVDs that are in this listing.

Harnesses (Pam's favorite ones)
1. X Back Sledding Harness from www.blackicedogsledding.com
2. My leather tracking harness from www.pamdennison.com

Hearts United for Animals: Puppy Mills
www.hua.org/Prisoners/Puppymills.html

International Association of Animal Behavior Consultants (IAABC)
www.iaabc.org
Great place to find a trainer and behavior consultant.

Laser pointers/lights as toys (BAD!)
http://healthypets.mercola.com/sites/healthypets/archive/2013/10/02/pet-laser-toys.aspx

National Association of Treibball Enthusiasts
www.nationaltreibball.com

NaturalRearing.com
www.naturalrearing.com
Information on raising your dog the natural way.

North American Dog Agility Council
www.nadac.com
One of the registries for agility.

Pet Professional Guild
http://www.petprofessionalguild.com
The Association for Force-Free Pet Professionals

petswelcome.com
www.petswelcome.com
A listing for hotels that accept pets.

Positive Motivation Dog Training
www.pamdennison.com
My website. Articles, class schedules, online classes and products

Puzzles
www.nina-ottosson.com
You can also do a google search for her puzzles. My favorites - the Tornado,
DogBrick and The Finder

SitStay
www.sitstay.com
A great source for the books listed here, plus other pet gear.

Stacy's Wag'N'Train
www.wagntrain.com
Super site with fantastic information about training and behavior.

Tawzer Dog Videos
www.tawzerdogvideos.com
A great source for great DVDs - including some of my own

Thensome pet health: vaccinations
www.thensome.com/vaccinations.htm
Information about vaccinations and how they really aren't needed as often as
veterinarians recommend.

Therapy Dogs, Inc.
www.tdi-dog.org
Another registry for Therapy Dog work.

United Kennel Club
www.ukcdogs.com

United States Dog Agility Association
www.usdaa.com
Another registry for agility.

World Canine Freestyle Organization
www.worldcaninefreestyle.org
Another registry for freestyle (dancing with your dog).

Finding a Positive Trainer

So you're hooked on positive but want some help with the details. There are as many trainers out there with all different levels of expertise and knowledge about learning theory as there are blades of grass. Ask five trainers the best way to train and you'll get 500 different answers. Many trainers think they are positive; they may use a clicker, but they also use a prong collar. This is not positive. This is punishment paired with food.

You'll need to interview your prospective trainer, and these are the questions you should ask:

> How long have you been training?
>
> What training organizations do you belong to?
>
> Do you compete in any dog sports? (Not all that important, but I would want to know.)
>
> What "tools" do you use? (If the answer is prong collars, head halters, and choke collars, run away.)
>
> You can even ask pointed questions such as these:
>
> If the dog jumps or bites, what would you recommend? (If the answers are in any way violent or hands-on, run away.)
>
> Can I have references? (Be sure to check them out.)

Ask to observe a few classes. Talk to students after the class. If what you see in the class is disturbing to you, don't join the class. It may take a while and you may have to drive a farther distance than you wanted to, but finding a positive trainer for your best friend will be the best investment you can possibly make.

Pam also offers Instructor Training Courses and certification for:

• Training the Whistle Recall

• The R.E.W.A.R.D. Zone for aggressive & reactive dogs

If you are a trainer reading this book and would like more information on developing a curriculum or tweaking your existing curriculum for teaching group classes, please contact me directly through my website.

   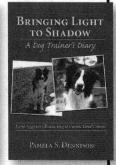
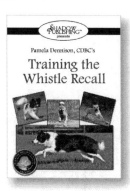